WATERSIDE WALKS

In Northumberland

Stuart Miller

COUNTRYSIDE BOOKS
NEWBURY, BERKSHIRE

First published 2008
© Stuart Miller 2008

COUNTRYSIDE BOOKS
3 Catherine Road
Newbury, Berkshire

To view our complete range of books,
please visit us at
www.countrysidebooks.co.uk

ISBN 978 1 84674 074 9

Maps by Gelder design and mapping
Photographs by the author

Designed by Graham Whiteman
Produced through MRM Associates Ltd., Reading
Printed by Information Press, Oxford

*All material for the manufacture of this book
was sourced from sustainable forests*

Contents

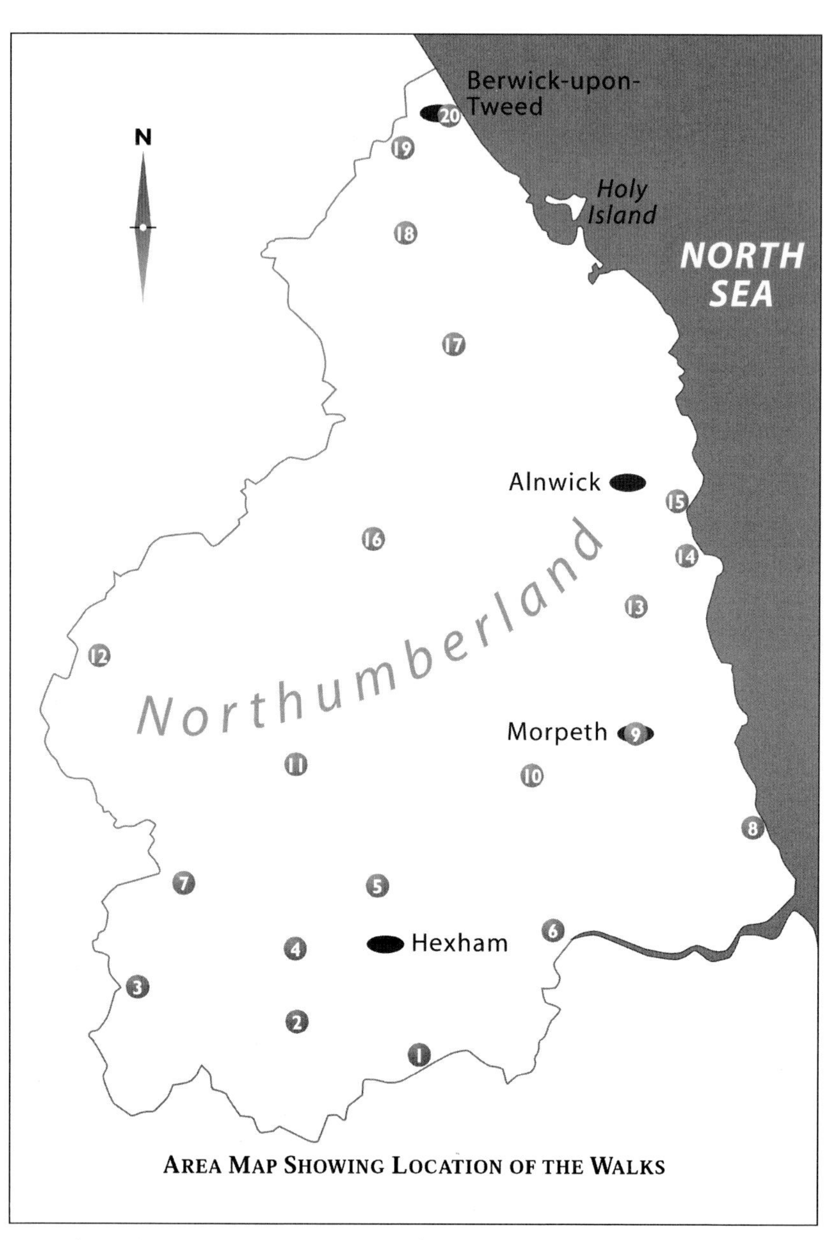

AREA MAP SHOWING LOCATION OF THE WALKS

Walk

PUBLISHER'S NOTE

We hope that you obtain considerable enjoyment from this book; great care has been taken in its preparation. Although at the time of publication all routes followed public rights of way or permitted paths, diversion orders can be made and permissions withdrawn.

We cannot, of course, be held responsible for such diversion orders and any inaccuracies in the text which result from these or any other changes to the routes nor any damage which might result from walkers trespassing on private property. We are anxious though that all details covering the walks are kept up to date and would therefore welcome information from readers which would be relevant to future editions.

The simple sketch maps that accompany the walks in this book are based on notes made by the author whilst checking out the routes on the ground. However, for the benefit of a proper map, we do recommend that you purchase the relevant Ordnance Survey sheet covering your walk. The Ordnance Survey maps are widely available, especially through booksellers and local newsagents.

INTRODUCTION

Northumberland is known as the 'land of singing waters' for good reason. It has relatively few natural lakes and no canals. It does have many rivers, however. There are three major river systems that have shaped the Northumbrian landscape and dominated its history: the Tyne, originating in the Pennines, and its tributaries; the rivers and streams radiating from the Cheviots; and the Tweed, with its tributaries, rising in the Southern Uplands, which marks much of the English and Scottish border. These awesome rivers will be your close companions as you walk in Northumberland.

The banks of the South Tyne and its tributaries, especially the Allen, are most attractive and inviting on calm, sunny days, although Pennine rivers are very prone to flooding quickly and dramatically. The Tyne, a veritable Jekyll and Hyde, travels a shorter distance than most rivers between source and mouth, and has a steeper slope. Unlike their Pennine originated brethren, the rivers rising in the Cheviots tend to be less destructive. Geology has produced soils that are better drained so, despite steep slopes, there are longer delays from rainfall to river flow. However, because of the vast quantities of sediment dumped in the valley floors by the Ice Age, there is great scope for the rivers to move laterally and constantly remodel their beds. The Cheviot rivers hold a record for moving silt and eroding banks and river beds on a scale not equalled elsewhere in England and Wales. These are amongst the oldest mountains on earth, and with the walk along the banks of two of the bubbling Cheviot burns, Carey and Coldgate, you come very close to them.

Northumberland also has the largest man-made lake in Britain – at Kielder – set in the most extensive man-made forest in Europe. Any book of waterside walks in the county must include a walk by Kielder. Nor could the Roman Wall be neglected. It has only a brief encounter with the North Tyne, at Chollerford, but is notable for four glacial loughs in the most scenic central portion. Similarly, Bolam Lake may be small but it is very attractive and the area is rich in features of historical interest. Northumberland also possesses a lovely coastline with superb beaches. No sandcastle builder worth the name should bypass Embleton, Bamburgh or Alnmouth beaches. Two walks in this collection – at Alnmouth and Seaton Sluice – include good sections along the coast.

This really is a region of superlatives. Next to Yorkshire, Northumberland is the largest county of England. It is the northernmost too. Much of it is far to the north of a large part of Scotland because of the oblique nature of the border. The ancient Saxon Kingdom of Northumbria in its golden age once extended as far north as East Lothian. Scottish kings briefly ruled as far south as North Tynedale. For three hundred years Northumberland was fought over by English and Scottish, officially and unofficially, until in 1603 the uniting of the two crowns ended division and the 'Debateable lands' were no longer under debate. As a result of this bloody past, the county also has one of the highest densities of castles and fortified houses in the country. On many of these walks you will discover peles, bastles and great castles and the names of some of the families who built them – and these names are often remembered on the inn signs that you will see.

Northumberland is one of the most rapidly developing tourist destinations in England. In various recent studies and league tables it has been identified as the most tranquil, the least densely populated, least spoilt, least light-polluted county in England and the county with the friendliest people (I made that one up – but they would win if there was a study). However, Northumberland is also a land of paradox. Amidst modern Arcadian scenery you will find areas that were once significant industrial landscapes. Comely Allendale was formerly the lead capital of Britain. Blanchland still bears the marks of lead mining. The rural lower Tyne valley of engraver Thomas Bewick was covered in a network of waggonways carrying coal from collieries along its banks to rendezvous with colliers in Newcastle harbour. Seaside Seaton Sluice was the centre of a huge industrial complex of glass and bottle manufacturing. The peaceful Bellingham area was heavily scarred by quarrying and iron manufacturing. You'll pass a small colliery in Kielder Forest and, even in the midst of the gentle rural ramble from Felton, you will encounter the remains of a former iron works at quiet Guyzance.

These twenty walks throughout Northumberland will give you a flavour of the appearance and character of the Ancient Kingdom. They will also be journeys through time, with companions drawn from the vivid tableaux of the history of the border county.

Hopefully, you will also find a little time to sample some of the numerous excellent inns and teashops that will be encountered during your expeditions.

Enjoy your walks.

Stuart Miller

BLANCHLAND AND THE DERWENT

From delightful Blanchland, follow the bubbling Derwent, enjoy excellent views over the famous Derwent Reservoir, then return across quiet pastureland and through woodland, passing signs of the lead industry.

Blanchland Bridge

Blanchland stands on the banks of the River Derwent. The name is commonly attributed to the white robes of the monks of the monastery, founded in 1175, but *Blanchland* means *white glade*. The church comprises the chancel, crossing and north transept of the monastic church. It contains interesting tomb covers, including that of Egylston, forester to the abbots, whose calling is indicated by the carved sword, arrow and horn. This area was noteworthy for lead and fluorspar mining, and evidence of industry survives. In his guide of 1888, William Weaver Tomlinson describes Blanchland as: '. . . a quaint old village beautifully situated on the banks of the Derwent, about two miles below the source . . . The stream is luxuriantly fringed with trees and shrubs, and the charming valley through which it runs contrasts strikingly in its fertility with the desolate hills.'

There is a story that during a Scottish raid the monks accidentally attracted the reivers, lost in a mist, by ringing their bells in the joyful belief that they had gone away. Hearing this from the hill known as Dead Friars' Hill, the Scots set fire to the buildings, looted the monastery and killed the monks. A similar account is also attached to Brinkburn Priory near Rothbury – but why waste a good tale!

The Derwent is named after the oak trees along its banks (Celtic *derva*, meaning *oak*). Tod Hill is named after the foxes that frequented it; the word *tod*, very common in place-names, means *fox*.

The Georgian Lord Crewe Arms, passed at the outset of the walk, was once the lodge of the Abbot of Blanchland and the abbey guesthouse. The garden was the cloisters. The bar is in a stone, barrel-vaulted area, previously a storeroom. The Hilyard Room, with its huge fireplace, was a room used by the monks for bacon curing. The former south wall of the monastic church is the boundary between the inn garden and abbey churchyard. The inn is haunted by Dorothy Forster, niece of Lord Crewe, the Bishop of Durham, who rescued her brother Tom from Newgate Gaol, where he had been imprisoned for his part in the Jacobite rising of 1715. The main beers, which could help in ghost hunting, are Black Sheep, Boddington's and John Smith's. There is an excellent range of bar meals. Lord Crewe himself is unwittingly to hand as sponsor of an appetising tossed salad, alongside Cumberland sausage with black pudding, breast of chicken with mango sauce, rump steak and many other dishes, including a children's selection.

Opening hours are from 11 am to 11 pm. Coffees are available from 10 am to 12 noon. Bar lunches are served from 12 noon to 2 pm; afternoon teas from 2.30 pm to 5.30 pm; bar meals from 7 pm to 9 pm and dinner in the restaurant from 7 pm to 9.15 pm. Telephone: 01434 675251; website: www.LordCreweArms.com

- **HOW TO GET THERE:** Blanchland stands on the B6306, which links with the A69 at Hexham in the north and via the B6278 to Consett in the east and the A689 to Alston in the south. The Lord Crewe Arms stands in the centre of the village.
- **PARKING:** Park in the main (free) car park on the north edge of Blanchland on the lane to Shildon.
- **LENGTH OF THE WALK:** 5½ miles. Map: OL 43 Hadrian's Wall, Haltwhistle and Hexham (GR 966503).

The Lord Crewe Arms' attractive garden

THE WALK

1. From the car park turn right and walk down to the Lord Crewe Arms, going over the Corbridge/Stanhope road. Continue to the bridge but do not cross it. Walk down its left side, following a sign to Carrick. Turn left on the path alongside the Derwent, crossing a couple of ladder stiles and, at a three-way signpost, continue ahead for Carrick Picnic Site. Follow the well-marked clear path in and out of woodland, across plank bridges and stiles and up steps. At one point it diverts left into a field then winds round back to the river. Continue on in the same way until, finally, steps take you up to exit onto a road near a bridge.

2. Turn left along the road. Cross a road bridge at the bottom of Tod Hill. Keep on past a scenic lay-by. The road bends left and rises. At a footpath sign to Acton on the other side of the road, cross and go over a ladder stile onto a path along the right side of a wall. Go through a wicket gate. Follow a woodland edge grassy path. Acton Farm appears on the horizon. At a wall corner keep ahead, following a line of telegraph

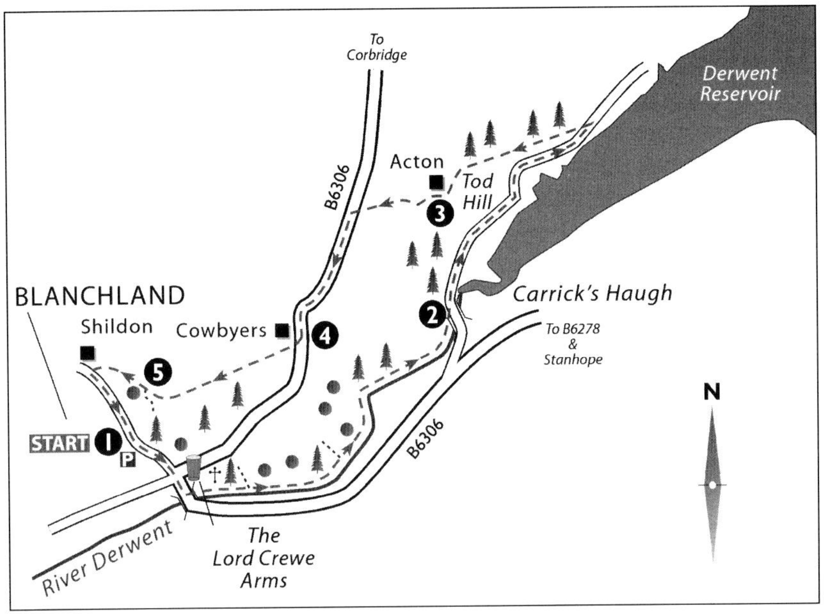

poles, and descend through gorse to a footbridge. Cross this and a ladder stile then walk up the bank to a telegraph pole. Head towards a field gate, following the fence on the left. Do not go through but turn left through an adjacent kissing gate. Bear left beyond it, crossing a track to go through another gate.

3. Follow the right field edge past Acton Farm. Go through another kissing gate, then turn left to cross a stile onto a track. Turn right and continue across a culverted stream. Just past this, fork right off the track along a narrow streamside path. Nearing a wall, follow it to the left up the bank to a gate. Go through this. Keep on with a fence on the left to cross a stile. Head half left diagonally across a field to a gate (signed back to Acton) and exit onto a road. Turn left along the road to Cowbyers.

4. Just past the old farm buildings, cross a stone wall stile on the right (signed to Shildon). Follow the wall on the right to reach another stile. Go over this into a small patch of young woodland and keep on with a wall to the right. Cross a stile then stay on the same line across a large field, following the right field edge and arriving at a kissing gate by a wide field gate. Go through and keep ahead, passing two marker posts, to reach and cross a ladder stile over a wall into coniferous woods.

5. Follow the track ahead. At a junction by a marker post turn right for Shildon. Go through a gate into a field below some cottages. The route veers round up to the right to exit by means of a gate to a stony track. Turn left along this and then left again onto a tarmac lane. Walk back down this pleasant lane to Blanchland and the car park.

PLACE OF INTEREST NEARBY
The **Allenheads Heritage Centre**, 8 miles south-west of Blanchland over moorland roads, describes the fascinating past and present of a small North Pennines lead mining village. Former mine buildings house interpretative displays, a blacksmith's shop of the time, a restored Armstrong pumping engine from nearby workings and a coffee shop (closed Monday). Behind the centre is a nature trail with some excellent walks. The Heritage Centre, Engine House and Blacksmith's Workshop are open daily from 10 am to 5 pm between April and October. Telephone: 01434 685395.

ALLENDALE AND THE EAST ALLEN

Allendale Town stands amongst spectacular scenery at the geographical centre of Britain. This walk takes you alongside the attractive River East Allen in an area still marked by the great lead mining industry that once made this one of the most profitable industrial areas in the country. Return via Catton and over quiet pastureland.

Allen Mill Bridge

Allendale's irregular market place is the scene of the famous Baal Fire celebration on New Year's Eve when 'guysers' dress up, blacken their faces and carry blazing tar barrels round the town on their heads. At midnight a huge bonfire is lit. The church of St Cuthbert (1873) is worth a visit. A memorial in the churchyard and Isaac's Well (1849) by the main road commemorate Isaac Holden, an itinerant tea seller, renowned because of his good works for the Allendale community.

In 1729 Sir William Blackett opened Allenheads mine. The Blackett mines once yielded a seventh of the lead ore produced in the UK.

But, by the later 19th century, the industry was declining. Allendale lost half of its population between 1861 and 1901. The Allen Mill abutment, which is passed on this walk, was part of the railway carrying refined lead from the Allen valleys to Newcastle. Allen Mill was a smelting mill where a huge water wheel drove crushing equipment. Huge furnaces burnt ore around the clock and underground flues took the fumes away to the Allendale chimneys about three miles away. The mill is now being restored.

The Allen is a Tyne tributary. The original spelling was 'Alwent' and probably meant *white* or *clear*. Catton could mean *wild-cat valley* since the earliest spelling was *Catteden* – so watch your back.

The King's Head in Allendale, originally part of a coaching inn, is over 300 years old. With its dark, intimate interior, stone floor, beams and a real fire in winter, it exudes character. It has a small, compartmentalised restaurant. Friendly staff contribute to the sense that this is a genuine village 'local'. The main beers are Jennings, Marston's and Banks's. Sandwiches and large filled rolls are available, as well as freshly cooked meals of fine quality. The menu is changed frequently and there is always a good range of fish, meat and vegetarian dishes, also tempting home-made sweets.

The pub is open from 11 am to 11 pm and food is served from 12 noon to 2.30 pm and 6.30 pm to 9 pm. Telephone: 01434 683681.

- **HOW TO GET THERE:** Allendale Town is 11 miles to the south-west of Hexham on the B6295, which links the A686/A69 and the A689. The King's Head is situated at the north edge of the market place.
- **PARKING:** In the market place (free).
- **LENGTH OF THE WALK:** 5 miles. Map: OL 43 Hadrian's Wall, Haltwhistle and Hexham (GR 837558).

THE WALK

1. From the King's Head turn right down to the East Allen bridge. Just before it, turn sharp right at a sign to Allenmill/Oakpool. Then embark on the riverside track, crossing a footbridge where water from the 4½-mile-long Blackett Level joins a stream entering the East Allen. Keep on past a ruined railway bridge abutment and across the road at Allen Mill Bridge. Follow the bridleway signed to Catton to pass sewage works on the right, then descend steps on the left to continue on the path closer to the river. Keep on over a stile and footbridges and through a wall gap by thick gorse. Cross another stile and follow

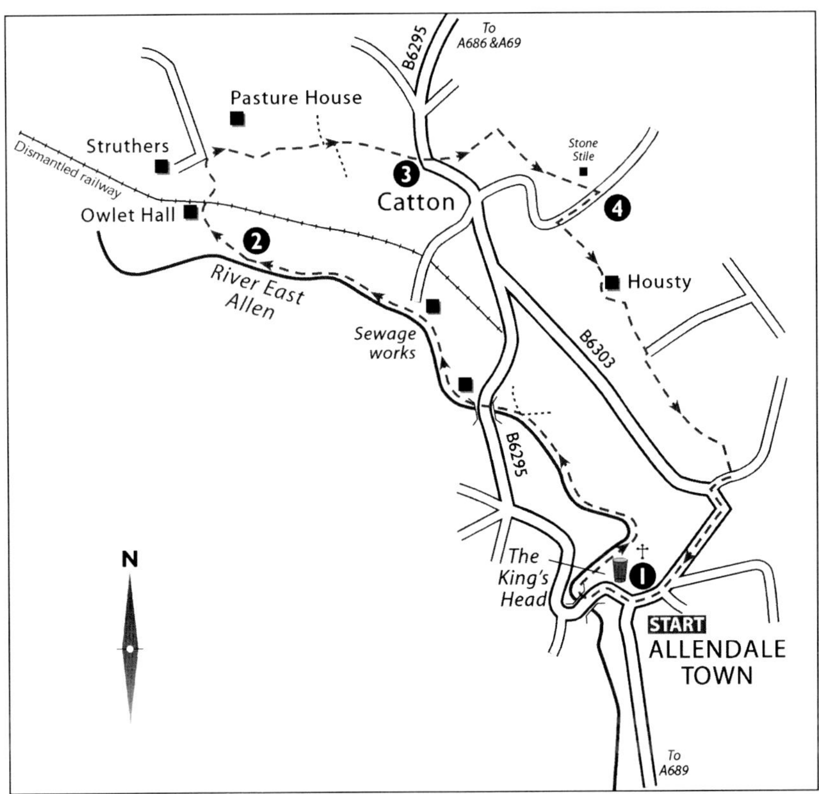

the narrow path as it winds through thickening woodland and crosses another plank bridge. You reach a flight of steps on the right.

2. Ascend these up the valley side. Exit into a field over a stile. Follow the left field edge to cross a ladder stile. Walk diagonally to the right over the field to Owlet Hall (a barn). Turn right at the barn through a gap in the fence. Cross the old railway track and turn right through a gate into a field. Continue diagonally up a steep slope to cross a stile and footbridge onto a track, joining a road at Struthers. At the three-way footpath signpost turn right to Catton through the metal gate. Bear half right across the field to cross a composite stile obscured by a bend in the wall. The farm on your left is Pasture House. Follow the left field edge to the wall end. Go left through one metal gate then sharp right through another. Follow the enclosed path to Catton. At the end cross a step stile and a footbridge then go between houses into Catton centre.

3. At the telephone kiosk cross the road to a sign to Stone Stile. Follow the lane through a metal gate, past a large cow barn then through another two gates and into a field. Walk across this to go over a ladder stile and then another field to a further stile. After the second stile, turn right and follow the wall on the right to a footbridge over Catton Burn. Then cross a high stone wall stile on the left. Follow a slight stream on your right up to a track. Turn right and go through a gate. Turn left to go through another gate then up to a stone stile. Head for the farm and cross a ladder stile to the right of the buildings. Bear left round the buildings to the drive and thence a lane.

4. Turn right down the lane then left at a sign to Housty, past a ruined barn. Bear round to the right of the farm and cross a stone stile on the left. Keep on left to a waymarked gate. The footpath has been diverted here. Go through into a field, then turn left and round to a ladder stile. Cross this and turn right to follow the wall on the right. Go through a gate onto a track. Turn right. Within yards, go through a gate on the left. Now follow a path over a very large field with the wall on your left. At a wall corner keep on, bearing slightly left to cross a ladder stile. Turn right, following the wall on your right, to cross a stile into a narrow path to a gate and exit onto Leadside Bank where you turn right to the main road. Go left to return to Allendale.

PLACE OF INTEREST NEARBY
The **North of England Lead Mining Museum** at Killhope near the junction of the B6295 and the A689 is well worth a visit. Attractions include guided tours, hands-on activities, a Mineral Exhibition, a working Armstrong waterwheel and the last pure red squirrel colony in County Durham. There is also a café and a shop. It is open daily April to October from 10.30 am to 5 pm. Telephone: 01388 537505; www.durham.gov.uk/killhope

FEATHERSTONE AND THE SOUTH TYNE

A two-level walk along the beautiful South Tyne then over the amazing Lambley Viaduct and back along the former railway track, now the South Tyne Trail . . . with a German Prisoner of War camp and a famous castle along the way.

Lambley Viaduct

Featherstone Castle dating from the 13th century is one of the most attractive of strongholds in the north. It was held by the Featherstone family for twelve generations and is famously haunted by a ghostly bridal party. Featherstone Park POW camp held German officers from 1945 to 1948. A hundred huts housed up to 7,000 prisoners. Only nine men escaped and when one of them drowned in the river seven returned to give themselves up and the other was caught by the local policeman. After the war many worked on local farms. They even had their own newspaper printed at Hexham, *Die Ziet am Tyne*.

The Lambley Viaduct was the final link in the Haltwhistle–Alston Branch Railway. Built by the Newcastle and Carlisle Railway Company and opened in 1852, it has been described as 'the most impressive monument of railway enterprise and optimism in the branch lines of Northumberland'. It carried lead, coal and limestone from Alston Moor on a trackbed more than 100 ft above the South Tyne. There are nine main arches, each with a 55 ft span, and seven smaller arches with a 20 ft span. The South Tyne Trail is 10 miles in length from Alston to Featherstone Park station.

The South Tyne rises on the slopes of Cross Fell. Delightful as the scene here is on a pleasant summer day, the Tyne is an ogre, flooding quickly and destructively. The high-arched Featherstone Bridge is the third version. Others were washed away in 1771 and 1782. Just upstream a gauging station records the speed with which the river rises and falls and gives early warning about the danger of flooding. There are actually several Tynes in the UK, the name coming from an innocuous pre-Roman word for *flow*.

The Wallace Arms is a stone-built, whitewashed country inn, with a beer garden in front of it. Inside you will find a small public bar, a restaurant area and a games room. It is stone-floored and has not been modernised out of character. The main real ales are Greene King Abbot Ale and IPA as well as frequently changed guest ales. There is an extensive menu with a good range of seafood dishes, grills and chicken dishes and an excellent steak and real ale pie, also vegetarian, children's and takeaway menus.

The welcoming Wallace supplies Sunday lunches virtually any time from 12 noon to 9 pm! It also does all-day breakfasts and has a full range of snacks and specials. In summer it is open all day with lunch served from 12 noon to 2 pm; afternoon tea 3 pm to 5 pm; evening meals 5 pm to 9 pm. In winter the hours are 12 noon to 3 pm and 6 pm to 9 pm on Tuesday to Thursday and 12 noon to 11 pm on Friday to Monday. Telephone: 01434 321872.

- **HOW TO GET THERE:** Featherstone is 4 miles south of Haltwhistle. Turn southwards off the bypass at Bellister and head for Park Village, thence Featherstone Rowfoot and turn right.
- **PARKING:** In the Featherstone Park station car park (free) near the Wallace Arms.
- **LENGTH OF THE WALK:** 6 miles. Map: OL 43 Hadrian's Wall, Haltwhistle and Hexham (GR 684607).

The footbridge over the South Tyne at Featherstone

THE WALK

1. From the Wallace Arms turn left down the road and turn right along the former railway, which is the South Tyne Trail, signed 'Park Village' and passing the Station House. Go through a gate and then along a deep cutting, between bridge abutments, through another gate and along the top of an embankment. Just before a bridge turn up left off the track alongside a hedge and through a wicket gate onto a road. Turn left through the attractive stone built Park Village then left again at a road junction. At a sign for Burnfoot go left down a path and steps and across a footbridge. Follow the left field edge. Stay with the path past a fence corner and as it descends then peters out in a field. Follow the same line towards the right end of a stone bridge. Exit up steps and through a kissing gate onto the road.

2. Turn left and on past Park Burn Foot farm along a very pleasant quiet lane. Keep on past Featherstone Bridge and then to Featherstone footbridge. Just past the footbridge go through a wicket gate on the right (signed 'Diamond Oak'). Follow the lovely grassy path by the riverside. At a waymarked post join a tarmac track and keep on through twin gateposts. Walk on along the track, which was the main road through the camp. Pass old concrete posts, the concrete bases of POW

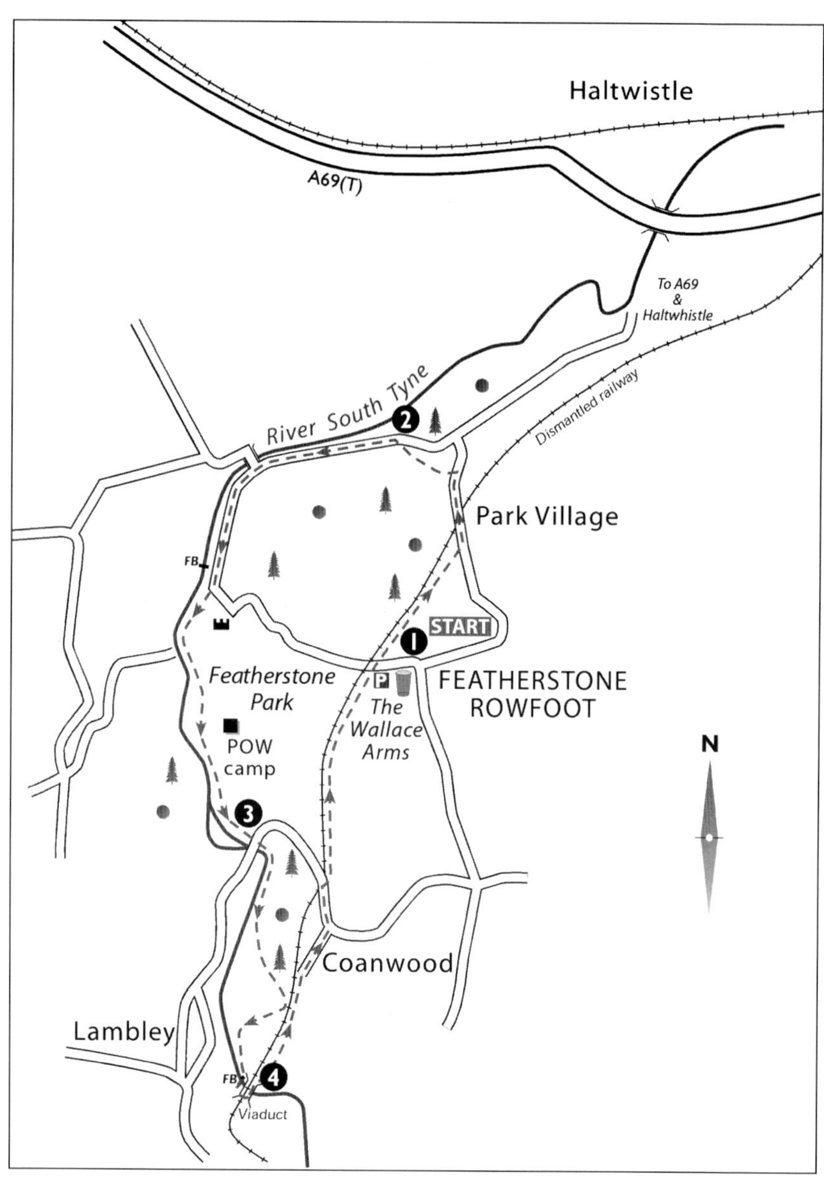

Haltwistle
A69(T)
To A69
&
Haltwhistle
River South Tyne
Dismantled railway
2
Park Village
FB
START
1
Featherstone
Park
P
The
Wallace
Arms
FEATHERSTONE
ROWFOOT
POW
camp
3
N
Coanwood
Lambley
FB
4
Viaduct

huts and some brick buildings. Keep on through a wide gate and near a modern road bridge exit onto the road via a wicket gate.

3. Cross the road and follow a sign to Coanwood through a wicket gate. Now follow a pleasant path with the river over on your right. Go over a small stream on a plank bridge and keep on. When the path peters out continue on the same line. Aim for an isolated house half left, crossing another plank bridge in a boggy area. Cross a rocky drive and go behind the house to walk over a small bridge. Go diagonally across the field to the far left corner by the river and pass through a wicket gate to follow the narrow woodland path with the river to the right. Soon the Lambley Viaduct looms above you. Cross an impressive footbridge on the right, climb the steps to the viaduct and walk over it.

4. Go through the gate then walk on along the track. Beyond a wicket gate cross another track to resume your walk along the railway track through a gate. Pass the station platform on your right and another big white house. At a wicket gate go over a road and keep on. Follow the track through a cutting under a bridge then through a kissing gate. Pass a pond over on the left. Go through another kissing gate then via another gate onto the road. Turn right up the road to the Wallace Arms.

PLACE OF INTEREST NEARBY
The **Roman Army Museum** at Carvoran, near Greenhead, just off the B6318 north-west of Haltwhistle, stands on the Roman Wall. Visitors can do a virtual journey along the Wall, join the Roman Army, dress up as a legionary or auxiliary and find out everything they always wanted to know about weapons, training, pay and recreation. It is open 10 am to 6 pm from April to September, and 10 am to 5 pm from mid February to March and from October to mid November. A joint admission price with Vindolanda (see Walk 4) is available. Telephone: 01434 344277; www.vindolanda.com

HAYDON BRIDGE
AND ALLEN BANKS

Starting by the South Tyne at Haydon Bridge, follow the trail of the famous biblical painter John Martin who was born at East Land Ends, passed early in the walk, in 1789. Continue westwards to the ancient and ornamental woods of Allen Banks, one of the treasures of Northumberland. The return is mostly along quiet lanes and across pleasant pastureland.

A delightful spot by the river

The Allen Banks and Staward Pele estates are in National Trust ownership. Between 1830 and 1860 Allen Banks was enhanced to give a 'wild' contrast to the formal parkland and gardens of the adjacent Ridley Hall, and 'Wilderness Walks' were added in the valley, with bridges, stone steps, an artificial pond, seats and summerhouses. The striking Staward Gorge was caused by the Allen cutting a steep sided valley, forming shingle banks, flats and cliffs. John Martin was much influenced by the dramatic scenery of the Allen valley and is famous for grand religious scenes set in dramatic landscapes. His paintings can be seen in the Laing Art Gallery, Newcastle and the Tate Gallery, London (visit www.wojm.org.uk).

The Anchor Hotel alongside the historic bridge was formerly a coaching inn. Part of it was once the courthouse of the Barons of Langley and it is first mentioned in 1422 when a felon was hanged in the courtyard. When the Earls of Derwentwater were involved in the Jacobite Rebellion of 1715 their estates were confiscated and given to Greenwich Hospital; in 1756 the name of the inn was changed because of this connection. The Admirals House, built for the receiving of revenues, is incorporated in the building. Bar meals may include steak in ale pie, Cumberland sausage, chicken goujons, ham and eggs, breaded haddock, scampi, cheese and broccoli bake, home-made lasagne, chilli con carne and steaks. There is also a children's menu. The Admirals Restaurant with fine views over the South Tyne offers a full range of dishes. The real ale is Theakston's.

Food is available from 11.30 am to 2 pm and 6.30 pm to 8.30 pm on Monday to Saturday; 11.30 am to 2.30 pm and 6.30 pm to 8.30 pm on Sunday. The bar is open from 11 am to 11 pm on Monday to Friday and from 12 noon to 10.30 pm on Sunday. Telephone: 01434 684227; www.anchorhotel-haydonbridge.co.uk

- **HOW TO GET THERE:** Haydon Bridge stands at the intersection of the A69 and the B6139. The Anchor Hotel is at the south end of the river bridge,
- **PARKING:** Roadside parking near the Anchor.
- **LENGTH OF THE WALK:** 9½ miles. Map: OL 43 Hadrian's Wall, Haltwhistle and Hexham (GR 844642).

THE WALK

1. From the Anchor turn right along Shaftoe Street. Where the road turns left, keep straight ahead down a lane (signed to Land Ends and Deanraw). Pass East Land Ends, John Martin's birthplace. Where the track bends left, keep on to Lees Farm through two gates. Turn left into the farmyard and between the farmhouse and cottages to a gate signed 'Allen Banks'. Go through the gate. Bear right across a stream and follow the grassy path as it turns left and then diagonally right across the field over a steep dip, past thick gorse and on to a ladder stile in the wall. Continue across the next field with woods to the right.

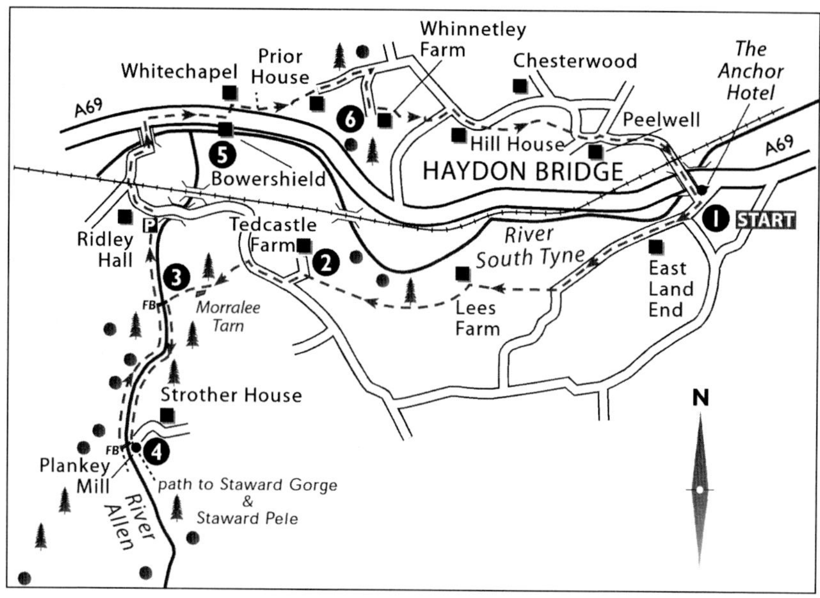

Go through a gate and follow the wall for a time. The path veers right to a ladder stile, which you cross. Bear half right to another stile by a gate onto the lane to Tedcastle Farm.

2. Turn left up to a junction then right and down to a gravel lay-by on the left and a National Trust sign. Go through a kissing gate then follow a track to enter woods by another kissing gate. Pass Morralee Tarn and at a waymarker opposite steps to the tarn, turn right and follow the path as it rises then descends, stepped in places. At a waymarked path junction turn right and follow the winding path down to the valley floor past blocks of stone. Near an overhanging crag on the left and a couple of waymarked posts turn right down steps then continue to the suspension bridge.

3. Do not cross but turn left and follow the riverside path, stepped in places, passing boulders and crags. At one point just before a flight of steps the path disappears sharp right between boulders; stay with it to go over a footbridge and emerge into a meadow. Cross a stile and walk on by the river edge. The path turns left into another field where you continue along the right edge. Keep on through a kissing gate near a ruin and join a road. Turn right to the bridge at Plankey Mill. (A little plank bridge and a stile on the left take you along the riverside path into dramatic Staward Gorge and up steps to Staward Pele – and back – if you have the energy.)

4. Cross the bridge. Turn right and follow the path back down the other side of the river through a small clearing, then on beneath high crags. Ignore paths to the left and keep right at a junction, passing the first bridge and arriving at Ridley Hall car park. Exit onto the road. Turn left and then right. Go under the railway bridge, then cross the Tyne to join the A69. Turn right and walk along the verge for about 300 yards to Bowershield, a large house beside the road.

5. Cross the A69 from Bowershield. This is a fast road and single carriageway at this point. Turn right along a track alongside the road, rising through a gate to join the drive to Whitechapel. Keep on through double gates, passing in front of the farm on the metalled drive, then keep on ahead and slightly left on a lesser track (signed Prior House). Stay with this through a couple of gates until it turns sharp left before another gate. Keep on through the gate. Follow the right field edge through another gate onto a rough track through woods to arrive at

Morralee Tarn

a road to Prior House. Keep on, then turn right to Whinnetley. Go through gates and follow the track round left past the house to go through a wicket gate on the right.

6. Walk across a field half left to go through a gate and over the next field to cross a sequence of two stiles separated by a footbridge. Follow the field edge round to the right. Before a gate cross a stile on the right. Go over a footbridge then follow the fence round on the left to cross a stile onto a road. Turn left, then right at a junction. Past a sharp left bend in the road cross a stile on the right (signed 'Peelwell'). Bear half left across the field then turn left, following the fence. Keep on through two gates to exit onto a road where you turn right to Peelwell. At a junction turn right and continue down to Haydon Bridge.

PLACE OF INTEREST NEARBY
Roman **Vindolanda**, 10 miles north-west of Haydon Bridge along minor roads, includes world famous civilian and military remains and on-going excavations, the Chesterholm Museum and several reconstructions of Roman buildings and a section of the Wall. There is a good café and shop. A joint admission price with Carvoran (see Walk 3) is available. Vindolanda is open 10 am to 6 pm from April to September, and 10 am to 5 pm from mid February to March and October to mid November. Telephone: 01434 344277; www.vindolanda.com

WARDEN AND THE TYNE

On this walk you encounter the Meeting of the Waters where the North Tyne joins the South Tyne. En route, walk alongside the pretty Coastley Burn, enjoy excellent views across the Tyne Valley and follow a stretch of the Tyne Green Trail, west of Hexham Bridge.

Watersmeet

There was a ferry boat on 'the boatside' here from the 13th century. In 1826 a suspension bridge was constructed and the old toll house can still be seen. The present bridge was built in 1903. The name Warden derives from *weard dun* meaning *watch hill* and the view from Warden Hill along the South Tyne Valley is spectacular.

The Tyne has the highest recorded flood flow on any river in England and Wales, and there have been many disastrous floods. It travels a shorter distance than most rivers between source and mouth, and has a steeper slope so the travel time of a flood wave can occur within eight hours of heavy rainfall. Near West Boat hamlet a marker stone indicates the level in 1771, thirteen feet above the normal level. Bridging the Tyne was a saga. When John Smeaton, 'the father of civil engineering', was approached to rebuild the bridge over the Tyne at Hexham he replied: 'I would beg you to consider whether you may not stand a better chance by employing some other able Engineer who has not got the Horrors of the River Tyne painted upon his imagination.'

The present Hexham Bridge (Robert Mylne, 1793) was the third attempt. Earlier efforts were wrecked in 1771 and 1782 (Smeaton's) by floods or quicksands. Even the A69 Constantius bypass bridge, completed in 1976, followed an earlier attempt that collapsed in 1975. You should be okay though! As you walk along the riverside Tyne Green Trail you pass the remains of a railway bridge that carried the Border Counties Railway, a branch of the Newcastle and Carlisle line, which went up the North Tyne valley. It was built between 1855–1862 and closed in 1956.

The Boatside Inn, at the start of the walk, offers Black Sheep, John Smith's, Marston's and Theakston's ales. The typical menu includes substantial and unpretentious food such as home-made chicken, steak and ale pies, a good repertoire of steaks and fish dishes, a tempting succulent lamb shank, oven-roasted duck breast and Californian loin of pork. Vegetarians are well catered for with items like thyme, lime and asparagus risotto and five cheese cannelloni. There is a beer garden.

The Boatside Inn is open from 11 am on weekdays and 12 noon on Sunday. Food is served from 12 noon to 2 pm and 6.30 pm to 9 pm (from 7 pm to 9 pm on Sunday evenings). Telephone: 01434 602233; www.theboatsideinn.com

- **HOW TO GET THERE:** Warden is just a couple of miles north-west of Hexham, off the A69. Coming from the east, turn right onto the B6319 and cross Warden Bridge, The Boatside Inn is at the north end of the bridge.
- **PARKING:** In the Boatside Inn car park (with permission of the landlord). Alternatively, on the roadside.
- **LENGTH OF THE WALK:** 7 miles. Map: OL 43 Hadrian's Wall, Haltwhistle and Hexham (GR 910660).

The Boatside Inn at Warden

THE WALK

1. From the Boatside cross the bridge and turn right past Toll Cottage. Walk along the lane, crossing a footbridge, to Coastley Burnfoot Farm. Just past this turn left through a gate and follow a path into woodland, going beneath a former railway bridge through a kissing gate. The path winds on to reach the A69. Cross this carefully to a drive and walk past Coastley Farm with Coastley Burn below on the left. The track bends left past a cottage. Go over a footbridge across the burn. Continue up the bridleway, signed to Low Gate, passing the entrance to Hackford Farm on the right. Ignore paths to the left. Follow the track to the left round a caravan site and to the right near cottages, then join a road at Low Gate.

2. Turn left and just before Fernstone House, cross a stone stile and go through a wicket gate by a signpost to Carlisle Road. Follow the right field edge to cross a stone stile. Walk along the left edge of the next field. At a path crossroads do not go over the stile but turn right towards Highside Farm. Cross a stile, go through two gates and pass in front of the farm. Go through another wide gate and keep on along

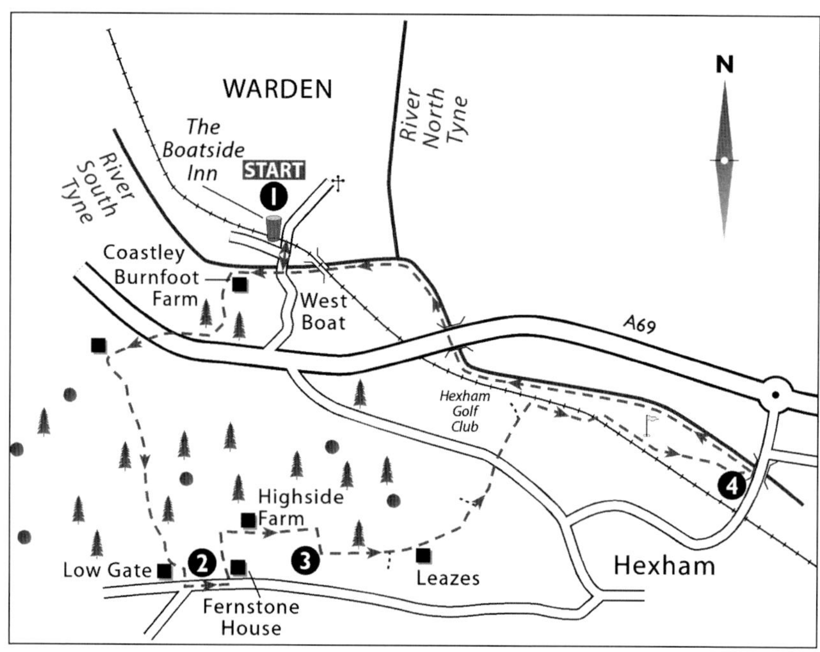

the left field edge. Cross another stile into the next field then follow the left edge to a locked gate into young woodland. Turn right and follow the field edge to a stile.

3. Cross the stile then walk alongside mixed woodland on a track, which becomes a lane, bending right by Garden Cottage and then left down Leazes Lane. Pass cottages and houses and Leazes Cricket Club on the left and arrive at Shaw's Lane on your left. Follow this past the end of Duke's Road then down a continuation stony track to a fast road. Cross this and go down the road to Hexham Golf Club. At the golf club entrance keep on down the earth track, Spittal Lane, which winds behind the clubhouse to the railway. Turn right and follow a lane with the railway embankment on the left. Approaching a playing field, go through a tunnel on the left then turn right along a narrow path with the railway on your right and golf links on the left. Cross a footbridge and walk along a road past the clubhouse of the Tynedale Golf Club then on past a play area and toilets to reach a café and the Hexham Boat Club House.

4. At the café turn left along the riverside path down a long avenue of trees then to a lane alongside the railway embankment. Continue between the river and railway, passing the remains of the piers of an old railway bridge. At a footpath sign on the right, descend steps and follow a path to Watersmeet beneath the A69 road bridge, then up onto a flood embankment. Turn right along the embankment and walk on past Watersmeet. At the embankment end descend onto a path with a fence on the left. Go beneath the railway bridge. The path winds round to the left beside Ferryman's Cottage and joins a lane at West Boat hamlet. Turn right and walk back to Warden bridge.

PLACE OF INTEREST NEARBY
Hexham Old Gaol was the first recorded purpose-built prison, constructed by order of the Archbishop of York in 1333. From then to the 19th century it housed thousands of prisoners. The Old Gaol is now a modern museum with hands-on displays and a vivid 'reiver raid' film. Explore the treatment and punishments of the prisoners in a medieval gaol, and experience the lives of the border reivers. Try on the costumes of the reivers, see the skull of Sir John Fenwick and pry into local secrets and family feuds. All quite scary . . .

It is open from 10 am to 4.30 pm daily in March to October, and on Monday, Tuesday and Saturday in February and November. Telephone: 01434 652351.

WYLAM AND THE TYNE

Things can't get much more historical. Setting off eastwards along the south bank of the Tyne to Ryton Willows and Newburn Bridge and then returning on the north bank, the route includes the site of a battle that triggered the English Civil War, the network of coal waggonways from which modern railways were born and the birthplace of George Stephenson, and it's all flat and easy walking as well.

Railway pioneer George Stephenson was born in this cottage in Wylam

The 5 ft gauge Wylam Waggonway, which you can see on the return leg of the walk, was built around 1748 and carried coal from Wylam Colliery to Lemington Staiths, thence onto keels and colliers. The railway pioneers William Hedley and George Stephenson lived and worked in this area. Both Stephenson and Timothy Hackworth were born in Wylam, Stephenson in 1781 in a cottage passed by the waggonway. He lived for part of his childhood in Newburn, where he also attended night classes. His father was a fireman working a pumping engine. Young George was engineman or plugman.

In 1808 cast iron plate rails replaced wooden rails. In 1812 colliery viewer William Hedley was asked by the Wylam owner Christopher Blackett to build a locomotive, and a test version was running in 1813. Steam locomotives were well established by 1815. Hedley followed Trevithick in using smooth wheeled engines rather than toothed wheels and cogged rails for laden wagons – a feature also used by George Stephenson, who visited Wylam to see Blackett's engines at work when he was living at Killingworth. Stephenson's first engine was constructed in 1814. Wylam Colliery closed in 1868 so the waggonway was little used and finally closed in 1966, reopening as a bridleway in 1972. Wylam's name derives from Old English *wil*, a *mechanical device* or *fish trap* (related to our modern word *wile*), and could mean a water mill on a water meadow (*hamm*).

Ryton Willows was very popular with Newcastle trippers in the early 20th century. There were swings and roundabouts, and boating and curling on the pond. The present ferry house replaced one washed away on the former Ryton Island. Newburn Boathouse Inn flood level marks show that in 1771 it was flooded to the ground floor ceiling. From 1850 dredging by the Tyne Commissioners resulted in greater depth and increased tidal reach so riverside villages beyond Wylam and Newburn are now safe from flooding. The Tyne is now pollution free – there are salmon and other fish in good numbers and occasional common seals.

The Fox & Hounds at Wylam is 'open plan' and has a relaxed atmosphere. Its real ales are Jennings and Black Sheep (note that just after the start of the walk you can sample even more – the Boathouse Inn beside the station boasts twelve real ales). A typical menu might include strips of beef fillet flamed with brandy and finished in stroganoff sauce, smoked fillet of haddock in grain mustard sauce, king prawns sautéed in garlic butter, and lamb shank braised in port and rosemary sauce. You get the idea . . . There is a good range of desserts as well.

The inn is open daily from 12 noon to 11 pm. Food is available on Tuesday to Saturday from 12 noon to 2 pm and 6 pm to 9 pm. Sunday lunch is served from 12 noon to 4 pm. Telephone: 01661 853246.

- **HOW TO GET THERE:** Wylam is signed off the B6528 from the A69.
- **PARKING:** Roadside parking or in a pay and display car park near the north end of the bridge.

- **LENGTH OF THE WALK:** 7 miles. Map: OS Explorer 316 Newcastle upon Tyne (GR 117646).

THE WALK

1. From the Fox & Hounds turn left and cross the bridge. Go left into the station car park at a public footpath sign to Clara Vale then follow a good gravel track. At a fork keep left along the Keelmans Way, a 14 mile cycling and walking route, alongside the golf course on the right. At the next fork keep left again. Pass the end of the golf course. Beside a level crossing keep on left again down past the Ferry House.

2. Continue through a gate (near an information board) into Ryton Willows then on through a kissing gate. Pass a meadow and a covered reservoir then another field to reach Newburn Bridge. Cross the bridge then turn left and walk in front of the Boathouse pub. Continue on past the Tyne Rowing Club then playing fields on your right. Cross a footbridge then follow the track round the edge of a car park, picnic site and children's play area. Keep on past a large boat landing. Stay on the gravel track off to the left along the river edge.

3. Opposite the Ferry House the path forks. Take the left fork. Follow a narrow path above the river. At a kissing gate keep on. The path crosses an open meadow area. You begin to see another golf course over on the right. Pass a marker post pointing to the waggonway but keep on the riverside path. It can be muddy and there are some sections

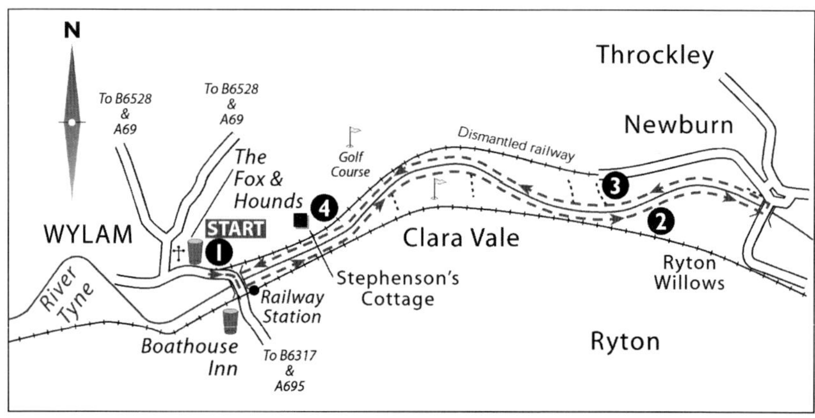

The welcoming Fox & Hounds pub

where erosion has brought it close to the river edge. Pass a wicket gate on the right then enter the Close House Riverside Nature Reserve. At a fork keep left. The path winds through the woodland then rises and widens. You now arrive at another kissing gate.

4. Go through the kissing gate into a clearing. Here, if you wished, you could turn sharp right and follow the path to your right onto the waggonway and visit the George Stephenson Cottage where the great engineer was born. Return to the path and continue on to go through a kissing gate and back into Wylam past a terraced row on the right.

PLACE OF INTEREST NEARBY
Cherryburn, a National Trust property, just off the A695 and 3 miles south-west of Wylam, was the birthplace of Thomas Bewick, Northumbria's greatest artist, 'Nature's engraver'. Here you can see his famous wood engravings of birds, animals and countryside scenes. Wander through the farmyard and enjoy lovely views of the Tyne Valley, relatively unchanged since 1760. Telephone: 01661 843276; www.nationaltrust.org.uk

ONCE BREWED, CRAG LOUGH AND GREENLEE LOUGH

Few walks combine a World Heritage Site, a Site of Special Scientific Interest and a name as curious as Twice Brewed! Spectacular views on the way out and quiet peacefulness on the return are the key words. The full route takes you along the Wall path and then on a section of the Pennine Way, before turning south-west through the wonderful Greenlee Lough Nature Reserve. The shorter circuit turns back at Hotbank Crags, circling to the north of Crag Lough.

Hotbank Farm and Crag Lough

The Wall loughs – Grinton, Crag, Broomlee and Greenlee were formed by the scouring effect of ice sheets during the last Ice Age, which also turned the volcanic basalt into crags.

Crag Lough is a shallow lake, being steadily filled by the deposition of organic matter. It was near Crag Lough that William Hutton noted, in 1801, a stretch of Wall up to eight feet high. Aged 78, he walked the Wall in both directions having already walked 600 miles from Birmingham via the Lake District. All the way he carried a bag, umbrella and inkhorn. One pair of shoes lasted him throughout. It was so hot that he often had to undo his waistcoat buttons!

Greenlee Lough is a Site of Special Scientific Interest and a National Nature Reserve. It is shallow but at 18 acres is the biggest natural lake in Northumberland. Post glaciation deposits of silt, which are gradually filling it, are covered with reed beds visible close at hand from a mile-long boardwalk. Around the fringes are mires of peat deposits. Like the other loughs it attracts large flocks of over-wintering wildfowl. Otters, roe deer and foxes are commonly seen. It is also notable for invertebrates such as damselfly and dragonfly.

The Twice Brewed is Victorian but there has been an inn in this area since the 17th century. It may be so called because this stretch of drovers' road was between two hills or 'brews'. In 1934 the YHA converted a nearby farmhouse into a Youth Hostel called Once Brewed to indicate less potent beverages! Real ales include Allendale Best Bitter, Barngate's Cat Nap, Geltsdale's Kings Forest and High House Brewery Sundancer. The same menu, with a good range, is available in both bar and restaurant. There is also a beer garden. It is open 11 am to 11 pm on Monday to Saturday and 12 noon to 10.30 pm on Sunday. The bar menu is available from 12 noon to 6 pm Monday to Saturday. The evening menu is from 6 pm to 8 pm Monday to Thursday, and until 8.30 pm on Friday and Saturday. Lunches only are available on Sunday from 12 noon until they run out! Telephone: 01434 344534.

- **HOW TO GET THERE:** Once Brewed is 5 miles east of Haltwhistle on the B6318.
- **PARKING:** Park at the National Park Centre car park (pay and display) or at the Twice Brewed pub, with the permission of the landlord. There is also the Steel Rigg car park (pay and display) nearby.
- **LENGTH OF THE WALK:** 8½ miles or a shorter circuit of 4½ miles, returning from Hotbank Crags. Map: OL 43 Hadrian's Wall, Haltwhistle and Hexham (GR 751668).

THE WALK

1. Turn right from the Twice Brewed pub along the road (take care) then left up a lane. Past the Peel Bothy on the right cross a ladder stile (signed to Hadrian's Wall and Housesteads) and go over a field to another ladder stile. Beyond this, pass through a wicket gate then cross a stile and follow a paved path and steps up Peel Crags, going through a gap stile. At the top cross a ladder stile then follow the Wall path, stepped in places, negotiating two dips, past Milecastle 39 and on to a third dip and 'Robin's Sycamore' (used in the film *Robin Hood, Prince of Thieves*), where the path crosses the Wall and rises to Highshield Crags. Across a ladder stile continue above Crag Lough (take care – there are sheer drops with no fence). Continue through a wood to exit via a ladder stile and keep on to cross another ladder stile. Go over a farm track and cross another ladder stile. Now follow a grassy path up to Hotbank Farm. *For the full walk, continue from point 3.*

2. *For the shorter circuit:* Go over a stone stile by a gate on the left and follow the track across the farmyard through another gate. Stay with the track to cross a ladder stile then turn left over a step stile. Cross a field to go over another step stile and keep on. At a footpath sign turn right to reach another ladder stile by a gate. Cross this and walk over the field towards a couple of barns. Pass the left enclosure corner and follow the wall on the right. At a gate cross a ladder stile and walk on past another barn on the right (Peatrigg). The grassy path now becomes a good track. Stay with this past Peatrigg Plantation and to a gate where you cross a ladder stile onto a road. Turn left and continue to Steel Rigg car park, thence to the Twice Brewed.

3. *For the longer walk:* Keep on past Hotbank Farm, across a ladder stile and on up the bank, passing a small wood. At the top, from Hotbank Crags, you can see the four Wall loughs. Keep on into another steep dip, Rapishaw Gap, and turn left across a ladder stile, signed 'Pennine Way'. Follow a grassy path half right over a field. Keep on to cross a ladder stile near a small enclosure then go over a track and follow the path parallel to a wall on the left. Cross another ladder stile and keep on across a small stream. Continue up a bank and round to the right. Cross a ladder stile onto a clear farm track. Go over this and cross another stile. The path winds left then

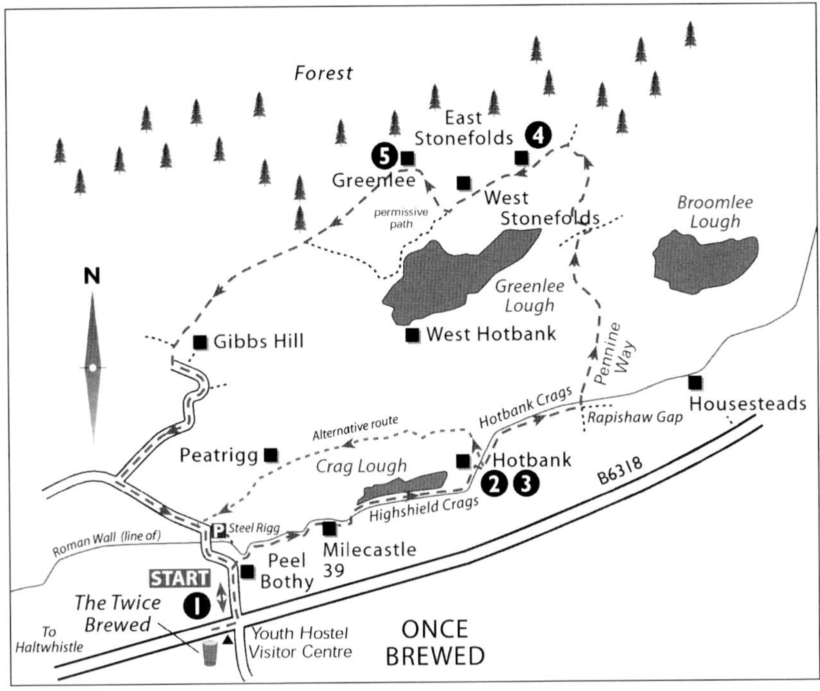

right, and rises. Making for the farm ahead, the vague path turns sharply to the right, then left to cross a ladder stile and footbridge. Follow the wall on the right to cross another ladder stile and descend a track at a sign to Gibbs Hill. Turn left to East Stonefolds

4. Go through a gate and pass the farm. Cross a ladder stile and follow the track, with Greenlee Lough on the left and thick woodland on the right. Go through a gate at West Stonefolds farm and pass in front of the house. Turn right to exit across a ladder stile. Turn left along a faint path, descending to walk over a footbridge. Cross another ladder stile then go on to a step stile near a sign to Greenlee Farm and 'Birdhide/Greenlee Lough'. The latter would take you via a waymarked path and a boardwalk through reed beds at the end of Greenlee, thence up to a good track where you turn left and on to Gibbs Hill – see point 5. However, **be warned** that the boardwalk can be impassable after heavy rain. Alternatively, turn right at the signpost to follow the path uphill with a wood to the right. Cross a ladder stile and keep on up a

Crag Lough seen from Milecastle 39

field then to the left in front of Greenlee Farm. Follow a track round to the right to a gate (signed back to the permissive path). Go through and on to a T-junction.

5. Turn left and follow this track, passing a sign on the left to the permissive path to 'Greenlee Lough/Birdhide' (the path you would take to join this track if you had followed the boardwalk option). Keep on, crossing a series of three ladder stiles to pass a barn on the left. Continue on through a wide gate, round to the left and on to a stone bridge near the drive of Gibbs Hill. Cross the bridge and follow a quiet lane, past a sign to Gallowshieldrigg. At a T-junction turn left and walk to Steel Rigg car park, thence back to the Twice Brewed.

PLACE OF INTEREST NEARBY
Housesteads Roman Fort, only a couple of miles to the east, in a dramatic situation at the most scenic point of the Roman Wall, is one of the most complete in Britain with its granaries, barracks, hospital and ingenious latrines. There is also a visitor shop and kiosk selling tea/coffee etc. There is a ¾ mile walk to the fort from the shop. Telephone: 01434 344363; www.english-heritage.org.uk

SEATON SLUICE
AND HOLYWELL DENE

From a unique harbour, this splendid route follows a lovely stretch of coastline to the eye-catching St Mary's Lighthouse, then field edges and an old railway line to return along lovely Holywell Dene, now a nature reserve. Easy walking all the way — and fish and chips at the Waterford Arms.

The huge beach stack known as Charley's Garden

In 1660 the local landowner Sir Ralph Delaval constructed harbour walls at what was then known as Hartley Pans to help with the expansion of his coal mining and salt-making enterprises. Sluice gates were added in 1690. At low tide the floor was scoured by horse-drawn ploughs and the loose mud was washed away when the gates opened. The name of the area became Seaton Sluice. On Sandy Island, hills were created from the ballast of collier brigs from London. The harbour entrance, also created in 1660, was prone to silting so the Cut was blasted out by Tom Delaval in 1761 to create a new entrance. Planks at each end formed one of the first East Coast wet docks. Rocky Island was then entered by means of a rotating wooden bridge, which enabled vessels to come through. Salt was produced there by evaporating brine in huge pans.

From 1763 to 1896 six great cones dominated the skyline at Seaton Sluice, a vital part of the successful glassworks that developed here. The works also included a brickyard, granary, quarry and four streets of houses. At its peak it produced 145,000 dozen bottles a year, which were loaded onto sloops via a short tunnel. Information boards tell you about the local industries and the fascinating harbour.

The huge beach stack is called Charley's Garden – supposedly after Charley Dockwray who had a vegetable garden on top! The cliff top at Curry's Point is one of the few remaining semi-natural grassland areas in North Tyneside. The prominent white lighthouse was in operation from1898 to 1984. It was the last to be electrified, in 1977. Before that it was lit by means of a wick burner run on paraffin, which was hoisted in cans to the top of the lighthouse by rope and pulley. Access is via a tidal causeway. It has a visitor centre and visitors can climb the lighthouse (open April to October daily and at weekends,

St Mary's lighthouse

Wednesdays and bank holidays from November to March. Telephone: 0191 2008550).

Holywell Dene is old ravine woodland along Seaton Burn. At the end of the 19th century William Weaver Tomlinson wrote of it: '. . . a charming place for a picnic, as the visitors to the sea-side have long since discovered . . . and in the upper part . . . where the branches of lofty trees over-arch . . . some exquisite little pictures of sylvan loveliness.' It has been a nature reserve since 2003.

The Waterford Arms replaced an earlier building in 1899. Susannah, Marchioness of Waterford was the granddaughter of Lord Delaval. She inherited the bottle works from her mother in 1822. The Waterford Arms is renowned for its extensive fresh fish menu, which comes as standard, medium, large or jumbo! The grill menu is also wide-ranging. You can enter another dimension with the enormous Waterford Seafood Grill and Waterford Seafood Feast – it might be better to share with a friend. In addition there are pasta dishes, salad bowls and special vegetarian dishes. The main beers are John Smith's and Newcastle ales. The pub is open from 12 noon to 11 pm. Food is available from 12 noon to 9 pm on Monday to Saturday and 12 noon to 4 pm on Sunday. Telephone: 0191 2370450.

- **HOW TO GET THERE:** Seaton Sluice is 9 miles north-east of Newcastle, on the A193. Heading north, cross the roundabout at Hartley, where the A193 links with the B1325 and, after a few hundred yards, turn right and follow the road to the Waterford Arms which is on the left.
- **PARKING:** Roadside parking beside the Waterford Arms.
- **LENGTH OF THE WALK:** 6 miles. Map: OS 316 Newcastle upon Tyne (GR 337767).

THE WALK

1. From the Waterford Arms cross the road and walk towards the Quality Hotel, passing an information board beside the remains of the rotating bridge mechanism. Walk to the left of the inn and onto the cliff top path. Follow this as it winds round to the right between fences behind houses. At the road turn left and walk along the raised footway. Paths on the left lead down to the beach but keep on to a footpath sign beside a bench, which says 'Coastline/Countryside'. Turn left onto a good sandy path.

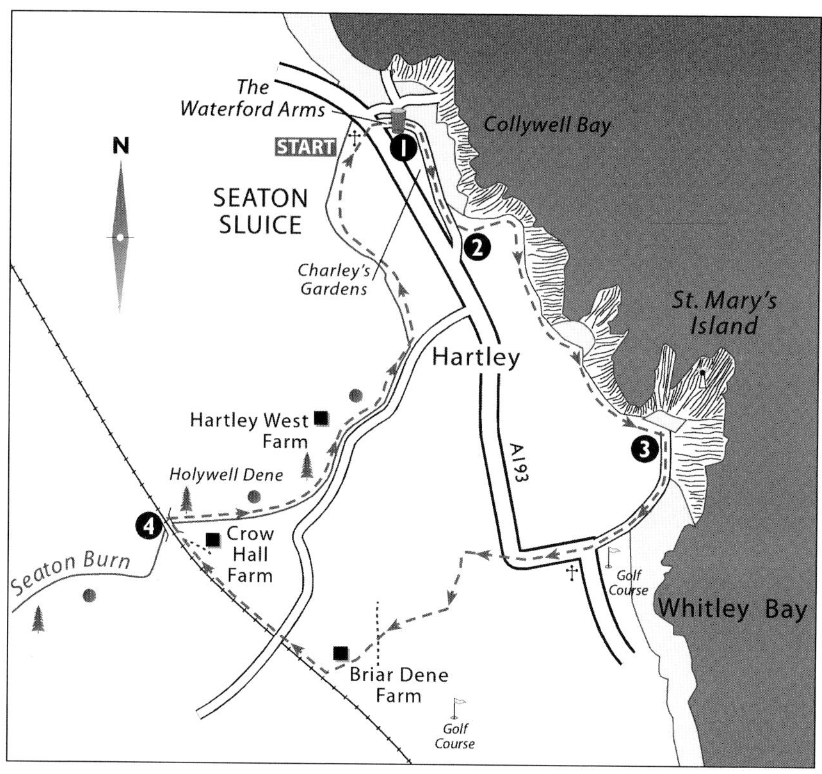

2. Follow this path along the coast, crossing a concrete track. Walk on past a caravan site. At a car park keep left to rejoin the path and follow it alongside a cycleway. Where the path forks take the left fork and keep on. Then follow a low fence round to the right and rejoin the path, which parallels the cycleway. Within yards follow it off to the left. At a fork at an information board about the coastal grassland, turn left. Go down the path, cross a footbridge and continue on to benches overlooking St Mary's Island. Descend steps to join a concrete path parallel to the road, and turn right along this.

3. Follow the road to arrive at the main road. Turn right and walk up to a sharp right bend. Cross over (taking care) and continue on a track alongside a golf course and between the abutments of an old railway bridge. Turn left past this and follow the field edge to a stile on the right, which you cross. Keep to the right field edge and go over a ladder stile into a field. Cross this to the left end of the buildings of Briar Dene Farm then follow the track round them. Where the track bends right keep ahead over the field to the right corner to exit by a stile onto the former Seaton Burn waggonway. Turn right and follow this under a road bridge then past Crow Hall Farm. It enters Holywell Dene and crosses a high embankment through which the burn is culverted.

4. Just past a 'Waggonways' sign turn right over a stile into the Dene. Beyond an information board follow the right fork to the Dene floor. Follow the burn on your right. Pass a footbridge and a noisy linn (waterfall). Take the right fork when the path forks. Go through a fence gap stile and keep on. Ignore paths joining from the left. At another fork turn right through another fence gap stile and follow the path to cross a stile onto a road by a bridge. Walk over this then cross a stile to rejoin the path. Follow it up to a path T-junction. Turn left and continue with the burn on your left. Pass a footbridge on the left and go beneath a water pipe. The path runs on past a meadow then saltmarsh land. Approaching the harbour, follow the track up a bank on the right and exit into Seaton Sluice past St Paul's church. Keep ahead over crossroads to the Waterford Arms.

PLACE OF INTEREST NEARBY
The **Blue Reef Aquarium** in Whitley Bay shows many of the fantastic creatures that live in the sea. You can see everything from giant crabs and lobsters to seahorses and sharks. There are 40 recreated displays. At the heart is a giant ocean tank where an underwater walk through tunnel affords incredibly close encounters with the beauty of an exotic coral reef. If you ever fancied confronting a sting-ray or cuddling a sea cucumber this is the place for you. There is a good restaurant as well, and a themed gift shop. Telephone: 0191 2581031; www.bluereefaquarium.co.uk

MORPETH AND THE WANSBECK

Starting in the ancient market town of Morpeth, follow the silvery Wansbeck through thick woodland, rich with birdsong, on very clear paths. The route crosses the river and then, after a short uphill stretch, returns by field edges along the top of the valley.

Morpeth Bridge

Morpeth stands on the former Great North Road, now the A1. A ford over the Wansbeck was protected by a castle on the steep ridge to the south of the river. In the 13th century one of the earliest medieval bridges in the county was built here and the settlement outgrew its rival Mitford. It prospered and even in the 16th century was described as 'a far fairer town than Alnwick'. The present three-arched bridge was built by Thomas Telford in 1831, but the abutments and piers of the medieval bridge support a pedestrian bridge. The town centre has attractive alleys, courtyards and fine buildings, including a Vanbrugh town hall. The Chantry near the 19th-century bridge houses the Tourist Information Centre and displays the work of local craftsmen. St Mary's churchyard contains the grave of Suffragette Derby martyr Emily Davison. Admiral Lord Collingwood also resided in the town, at least for his one year of leave between 1793 and 1810.

William Weaver Tomlinson says of this stretch of the river: 'The Wansbeck may be followed . . . by a sylvan path through the Lady Chapel Wood. The scenery, due to the harmony of wood and water, is of the most lovely character.' The Wansbeck's name is derived from the OE *waegn-spic*, meaning *a wagon-brushwood causeway*. Morpeth could be *path across the moor*, or *the murder path*! Shadfen is based on OE *scealda-fen*, meaning *shallow fen*.

The rambling Waterford Lodge Hotel is an 18th-century coaching inn next to Carlisle Park. A good range of draught and bottled ales is available and there is an extensive choice of bar meals, including pizza and pasta menus. In the restaurant you can sample such delights as herb crusted rump of Northumbrian lamb, seared fillet of Northern Counties beef, orange-scented tenderloin of pork and pan roasted fillet of turbot, followed by some excellent desserts. Traditional Sunday lunches are served.

The inn is open from 10 am to 11 pm on Friday to Saturday, and 12 noon to 10.30 pm on Sunday. The restaurant is open on Tuesday to Saturday from 6 pm to 10 pm. Bar meals are available from 12 noon to 2.30 pm and from 6 pm to 9 pm Monday to Saturday. Sunday lunches are available until 6 pm when the standard bar meals menu is resumed. Telephone: 01670 512004; www.waterford-lodge.com

- **HOW TO GET THERE:** From the south, leave the A1 at Clifton to follow the A197 into Morpeth. The Waterford Lodge Hotel is just south of the A197 bridge over the Wansbeck. Approaching from the north, leave the A1 on the A192 which takes you through Morpeth town centre. Follow the road across Morpeth Bridge and the Waterford Lodge is on the right.
- **PARKING:** Limited roadside parking. There is a large pay car park next to St George's United Reform church just across the bridge.
- **LENGTH OF THE WALK:** 6½ miles. Map: OS 325 Morpeth and Blyth (GR 201857).

THE WALK

1. From the Waterford Lodge cross the road bridge. Turn right and walk along the road to the Old Red Bull on the right. Passing it, continue down an enclosed public footpath past allotments, with the river on your right. At the end cross the road. Do not go through a gate but turn right and walk a few yards to a footpath sign to Whorral Bank/Cottingwood Common. Go up a flight of steps and through woods. Pass a track on the left then a residential care home on the right and take the right fork when the path divides. At a path crossroads turn right down to the road. Cross the road and follow the sign for Bothal.

2. Now follow a long stretch through extensive woodland with the river on your right. There are occasional steps and numerous small footbridges on the undulating path, which takes you beneath an impressive railway viaduct. Keep right at a T-junction and forks and stay close to the river, watching the edge carefully where there are steep sections of bank. The valley opens out and you pass a large mill weir then cross a large footbridge to arrive at a sawmill. Keep up a short lane to exit onto a road where you turn right and cross Shadfen Bridge.

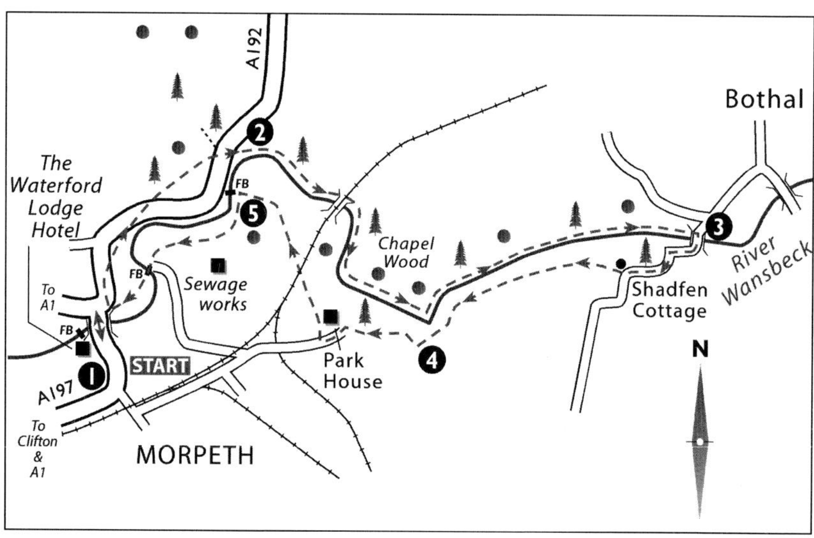

The mill weir near Shadfen Bridge

3. Follow the steep road up to Shadfen Cottage. At the cottage cross the stile, signed to Park House, and follow the right edge of a field, parallel to a private road and passing houses, caravans and sheds. Keep on past a waymarked post into the next field. Now follow the right edges of the next three fields, linked by stiles. The last stile in this sequence, with a rustic barn over to the left, takes you into a small field. Turn right and walk past former quarry workings. Follow the path at the right side of the meadow to cross a stile hidden round a corner and turn left into woodland.

4. Descend steps, cross a bridge then ascend steps and follow the path to the right into a field then across the middle onto a track, which joins a lane just past Parkhouse Banks. Keep ahead and just past a wide drive turn right at a footpath sign for Whorral Bank along a right field edge. The path goes through a gap on the right and onto a track. Turn left past a cottage and cross a hump-backed railway bridge. Continue across a field to go over a stile (or through the gap!) then follow the path over pasture and down into woods via a stile.

5. Follow the track to a T-junction of paths near a wooden bridge. Don't cross the bridge but turn left along the narrow riverside path and stay on this out of the woods and away from the river to a field where you follow the edge briefly then continue across the middle. Pass a couple of red-brick terraced cottages and keep on along a lane to a blue iron footbridge. Cross this and follow the lane back to the roundabout and the Telford bridge.

PLACES OF INTEREST NEARBY

Some 10 miles west of Morpeth is **Belsay Hall** (English Heritage). The beautiful 30-acre gardens link the medieval tower-house castle and Jacobean mansion ruins to the dramatic Greek revival Belsay Hall, built in 1807. There is a tearoom available in the summer months. Belsay Hall is open daily from 10 am to 5 pm in April to September and 10 am to 4 pm in October; in November to March it opens from Thursday to Monday, 10 am to 4 pm. Telephone: 01661 881636.

Alternatively, at the **Whitehouse Farm Centre** just off the A1 to the south-west of Morpeth you can feed and stroke animals to your heart's content! There is a good soft-play area, pedal tractors and tractor rides. It is open Tuesday to Sunday inclusive from 10 am to 5 pm except in January and November when it is open only at weekends, 10 am to 5 pm. Telephone: 01670 789998; www.whitehousefarm centre.co.uk

BOLAM LAKE

From a lake created by the most famous Newcastle architect, this varied and interesting walk leads you to the splendid Shaftoe Crags, then past the Piper's Chair and over the Devil's Causeway. The return to Bolam Lake and its visitor centre takes you alongside a medieval fortified house, with the opportunity to divert south to a Buddhist monastery if you wish.

Bolam lake

The Bolam Lake landscape was created from former bog land in 1816. The dam and the surrounding woodland were designed by John Dobson, later well known for his architectural work in Newcastle. After the Second World War, Bolam Lake was a popular countryside resort for Tynesiders and in 1972 it became a country park.

The once thriving village of Bolam has gone, but the church with its excellent late Saxon tower still survives. Harnham, just south of the route of the walk (see point 3), was also once a small village.

Shaftoe Crags, a site of ancient settlement, rear above the A696.

High on the crags is a large boulder known as the Piper's Chair. Salters Nick, which you go through, is below a former hill fort. Near the lane from Bolam West Houses is 'Poind and his Man', a round barrow with a grooved stone. The Roman unfinished road from Corbridge to Berwick, known as the Devil's Causeway, passes through this area. Shortflatt Tower, towards the end of the walk, is a good example of a 14th-century pele tower. It belonged to Robert de Raymes who owned Aydon Castle near Corbridge.

The Beresford Arms in Whalton (4 miles east of Bolam) is a long established inn, with an ivy-clad façade. The wide-ranging menu includes pub classics such as grilled Wallington Hall rib-eye steak and braised lamb shank. Among the 'Stevie's Wonders' are pan fried salmon and creamed potatoes, woodland mushroom and Parmesan risotto with pesto, honey roast breast of duck with caramelised apple, red cabbage and cognac cream sauce . . . and much more. Then there are the 'door-stops' (served from 12 noon to 2 pm on Monday to Saturday) such as 'the-big-pig-butty'. A board displays specials and mouth-watering desserts. Real ales include Black Sheep and Deuchars IPA. On weekdays and Saturday the pub is open from 12 noon to 5 pm and 6 pm to 11.30 pm and food is served from 12 noon to 2 pm and 6 pm to 9 pm. Sunday opening hours are 12 noon to 11 pm, with Sunday lunch offered from 12 noon to 5 pm and food available until 8 pm. Telephone: 01670 775225.

- **HOW TO GET THERE:** Bolam is about 8 miles north-west of Ponteland, just off the A696.
- **PARKING:** In Boathouse Wood car park (pay and display) near the Bolam Lake Visitor Centre.
- **LENGTH OF THE WALK:** 6½ miles. OL 42 Kielder Water and Forest (GR 085818).

THE WALK

1. From the visitor centre walk down to the lakeside and turn right on the path encircling the lake. Through the Pheasant Field clearing follow a length of boarding to West Wood car park. Bear right over this and follow the footpath through coniferous trees, crossing a wider track and several plank bridges. Exit onto the road near a sign to Harnham. Turn right and continue along the road, which has occasional fast-moving traffic.

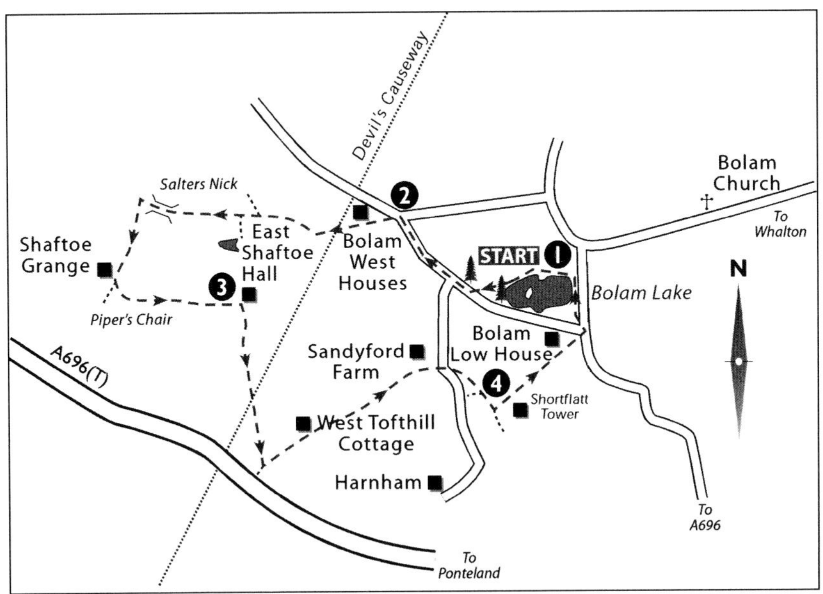

2. At Bolam West Houses turn left along a track to Shaftoe Crags. Entering a grassy area follow a wall on the right, with lovely views north-west to the Simonside Hills. Keep on through a gate and down a dry canyon known as Salters Nick. At the end of this the right of way follows the wall ahead and then round to the left to Shaftoe Grange. Alternatively, just cross the broken ground diagonally to the left to the farm. At Shaftoe Grange, turn left along a wide clear track. Over to the right is the unusual rock formation known as the Piper's Chair. Continue on over a stretch of imitation Roman road, through a gate and past cottages on the left and an old walled garden on the right to arrive at East Shaftoe Hall.

3. Turn right on a long path with a fence on the left initially then, through a gate, across a large open area, going over a footbridge and a ladder stile. At a road turn left and go through a gate past West Tofthill Cottage and on through another gate past Sandyford Farm on the left. At a fork turn right and at a sign for Belsay turn left over pasture (following the road would take you to Harnham Buddhist Monastery and Harnham Hall), aiming for Shortflatt Tower. Cross the footbridge and stile and go through a gate. Turn left and walk towards Shortflatt Tower.

Piper's Chair passed on the walk

4. Just before a gate cross a stile on the left into a paddock, then a footbridge. Follow the track ahead through a young plantation. Go over a ladder stile, then a step stile. Follow the fence on the right. Cross a footbridge into a field and then head diagonally towards a house on the right. Go over another stile into a paddock and cross this diagonally to a kissing gate at Bolam Low House. Turn left on the road and within yards turn right up a road to Whalton/Hartburn/Bolam. Turn left into the Low House Wood car park and follow the lakeside path round to the right to reach the main car park.

PLACE OF INTEREST NEARBY

The National Trust's **Wallington Hall**, 6 miles west of Bolam on the B6342 off the A696, was the family home of the prominent Blackett and Trevelyan families. Amongst numerous attractions are the famous Bell Scott paintings in the Pre-Raphaelite Central Hall. Discover the dolls' houses. Gaze at the Cabinet of Curiosities. Then venture into the splendid grounds and garden. There is a restaurant, a gift shop and a well-stocked farm shop. The grounds and garden are open daily all year round. The house is open daily except Tuesdays; 1 pm to 5.30 pm from March to September and 1 pm to 4.30 pm October. Telephone: 01670 773600; www.nationaltrust.org.uk

BELLINGHAM, THE REDE AND THE NORTH TYNE

Not one riverside but two! Set off over quiet pastureland and across the scenic hidden Rede Bridge to return along an old railway line, then by the edge of the lovely North Tyne to Bellingham.

Rede Bridge

Bellingham is a small market town on the North Tyne. This is one of many *ingaham* names, a compound of *ham*, meaning *homestead*, and *inga*, meaning *the people of* – in this case *homestead of the people of Bella*. No one knows why some Northumbrian names have a soft '*ga*' – '*Bellinjum*'.

The solid parish church of St Cuthbert illustrates the fear of Scottish reivers with its unique stone slabbed roof and narrow nave windows. Near the porch is the famous Lang Pack tombstone. It is claimed to be that of a robber hidden in a pedlar's pack left at Lee

Hall in Bellingham in 1723 to enable him to open the door to his colleagues. A suspicious servant noticing movement fired into the pack with a gun. When a silver horn found in it was blown, horsemen galloped into the courtyard expecting to find the hall opened but the defenders repulsed them. Only the body of the anonymous pack dweller was left behind.

The North Tyne and the Rede meet near Bellingham. The former originates from the Cheviots and has been harnessed and controlled by the great Kielder Water. The Rede is a meandering stream with gentle slopes and a wide flood plain. Like the Coquet (see Walks 13, 14 and 16) it is occasionally ruddy in colour and is called 'the red river' as well. If you have the time, you might wish to visit the Hareshaw Linn, 1½ miles north of Bellingham and reached by means of a clear path starting from the small bridge crossed on the way to the Heritage Centre. This is a Site of Special Scientific Interest notable for its beautiful waterfall, rich diversity of wildlife and luxurious mosses and lichens. It was once an industrial landscape but the works closed in the 1850s and now it is a peaceful scene populated by red squirrels, dormice, dippers and wood warblers. Near the Linn the Victorians built a bandstand on a terrace and held parties and picnics.

The family-run Cheviot Hotel stands in the town centre. It is stone built and beamed, with a real fire in winter. There is a restaurant as well as meals being served in the bar and lounge. Beers are John Smith's, Worthington and a local Auld Hemp from the High House Farm Brewery. Good solid bar lunches include various meat, chicken and fish dishes and a substantial all day breakfast. A wide range of sandwiches, burgers and jacket potatoes is offered and a comprehensive takeaway menu is available in the evening There is also a popular Sunday lunch carvery. It is open daily from 12 noon to 3.30 pm and 7 pm to midnight. Food is served from 12 noon to 2 pm and 7 pm to 9 pm. Takeaways are available from 7 pm to 10 pm. Telephone: 01434 220696; www.thecheviothotel.co.uk

The Fountain Cottage Tearooms, in the same building as the Tourist Information Centre in Main Street, provides breakfasts, snacks, sandwiches, lunches, afternoon teas and takeaways. They are open daily from 9.30 am to 6 pm on Monday to Friday and 9 am to 6 pm Saturday and Sunday. Telephone: 01434 220707.

- **HOW TO GET THERE:** Bellingham is 14 miles north of Hexham on the B6320. Follow the B6320 into Bellingham and past the Cheviot

Hotel on the left. Turn right on a road to West Woodburn, cross the Hareshaw Burn over a small bridge, then follow a left road fork. The Heritage Centre is on the right in the old railway station yard.

- **PARKING:** At the Heritage Centre in Old Station Yard.
- **LENGTH OF THE WALK:** 6½ miles. Map: OL 42 Kielder Water and Forest (GR 842838).

THE WALK

1. From the car park cross the road and turn right along a raised walkway to exit at the road where you turn left. Be careful and keep well in. When it swings right near a raised covered reservoir cross over to a gate signed 'Pennine Way'. Go through and walk towards Blakelaw Farm through two more gates. At the farm there is a track junction. Turn right and keep on through two gates to exit onto a road – be prepared for occasional fast traffic. Turn left. At a sign on the right to Rede Bridge follow a track down to Rawfoot Farm.

2. Turn right to pass in front of the farm. At the end of the buildings walk through a metal gate and at a wall corner turn left and follow the track by the wall as it goes left round the wall corner. Continue

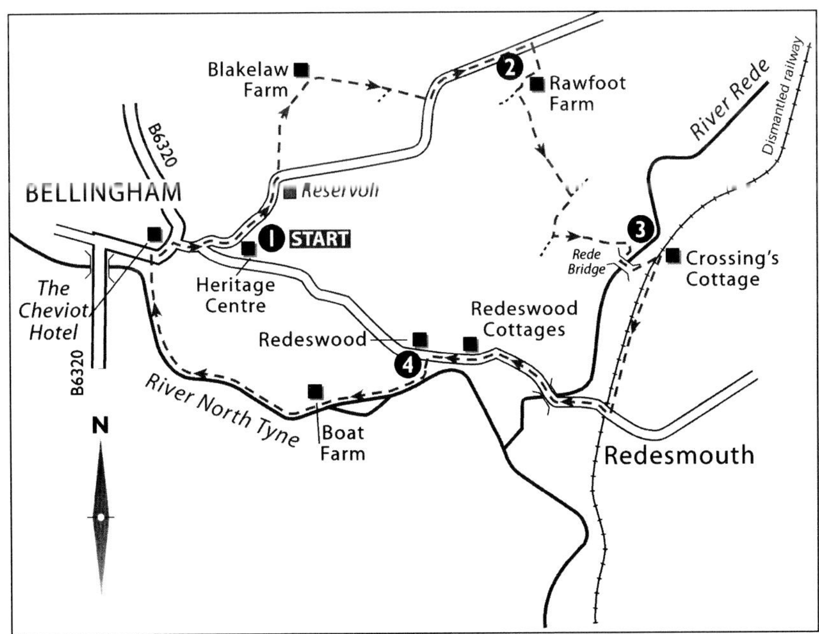

ahead with an avenue of trees on the right. Pass through a facing gate (signed 'public bridleway') and follow the right field edge through another gate. The track disappears but stay on the same line across pasture to a marker post and a track junction. Turn right to go through another gate and to another track junction. Turn left and follow the track as it winds round to the scenic Rede Bridge.

3. Cross the bridge and follow the winding track up to a cottage with a clever pheasant topiary. Turn right and cross a stile to join an old railway track to 'Reedsmouth' (sic). Follow this, crossing a couple of stiles. The track goes beneath a bridge but turn off right up to a road and Redesmouth. Turn right and cross the bridge over the Rede. Walk ahead under an old railway bridge and past Redeswood Cottages. Just before Redeswood cross the road to a footpath sign. Go through a gate and follow a track to the riverside.

4. At the bottom turn right to follow the North Tyne riverside path back to Bellingham. Cross a stile, which takes you onto a permissive path alongside a fence on your right (the actual right of way is on the other side). Exit at Boat Farm and follow the track in front of the farm. Go through a kissing gate on the left then skirt the edge of a private garden at Riverside. Keep on through a series of three wicket gates and past another garden edge. Leave the riverside path at a sign back to Boat. Turn left on a road and cross a bridge. Turn left and, by a garage, turn right along a path to 'Cuddy's Well' and up steps to turn right along a path. At the end turn left up to the main road. Turn right past the Cheviot Hotel and right again down the road to Redesmouth/West Woodburn and the Heritage Centre.

PLACE OF INTEREST NEARBY
Bellingham Heritage Centre is in the grounds of the former railway station just a few hundred yards from the village centre. Exhibitions include the Border Counties Railway, the evocative photographs of the 1920s and 1930s of W. P. Collier, the mines and quarries and the border reivers. Family history researchers can access a database of over 30,000 names. Using an old red telephone box you can dial and listen to the oral reminiscences of local people. You can even try on the helmets of border reivers for size! Telephone: 01434 220050; www.bellingham-heritage.org.uk

FALSTONE AND KIELDER WATER

The largest man-made lake in the UK, amidst the largest man-made woodland in Europe, is the focus of this walk through woodland and a secluded water meadow, concluding with a lovely riverside section. All this and a sculpture trail . . .

Kielder Water

William Weaver Tomlinson said of Falstone in 1888: 'This rustic village, situated in the midst of green haughs and trees, forms a pleasing contrast with the bleak fells around it.' This was always a stock farming area where drovers travelled ancient roads. Border warfare was a way of life and there are numerous fortified peles and bastles. The extent of wild moor is less nowadays, but the reservoir at Kielder Water has brought with it many other assets. Industries in the 19th century included coal mining and limestone quarrying. In 1920 the Forestry Commission arrived. The Victorian tourists who came here to enjoy the walking came by rail as well as road because Falstone station stood on a line connected to the Hexham–Morpeth line of the North British Railway via the Riccarton junction.

Kielder's name is derived from the Kielder Burn, 'the violent stream', which joins the Deadwater Burn to form the North Tyne. Kielder Water was planned in the 1960s with the intention of supplying a booming industrial economy and was opened in 1982. It has a shoreline of 27½ miles. Industrial decline made it somewhat of a white elephant but in recent years it has come into its own. Whatever the climatic conditions it is always at high levels and it supplies the north-eastern conurbations. It is also one of the region's major tourist venues with over 250,000 visitors a year.

The popular family-owned Pheasant Inn at Stannersburn was originally a farmhouse and stands in a small group of cottages. The 17th-century building has two comfortable bars, with wood panelling, original beams and cosy open fires in winter. Its walls are covered with historic photographs tracing the development of the local community. The brass beer taps gleam and anything wooden is polished to perfection. The real ales are Timothy Taylor's Landlord, Wylam Turbinia and Whistle Stop. A full range of food is served, from sandwiches and salads to substantial bar meals using local meat, fish and vegetables. The Pheasant is especially famous for slow-roasted Northumberland lamb, baked gammon with Cumberland sauce and home-made game and steak and kidney pies. It is open in summer from 11 am to 3 pm and 6.30 pm to 11 pm; Sundays 12 noon to 7 pm. In autumn and winter the hours are 12 noon to 2.30 pm and 7 pm to 11 pm. Food is available seven days a week from 12 noon to 2 pm and 7 pm to 8.30 pm. Telephone: 01434 240382; www.thepheasantinn.com

The Falstone Tearooms in the modernised old school building serve a good range of food and beverages. They are open Easter to October seven days a week from 10.30 am to 4.30 pm. Winter times are Thursday to Monday, 11 am to 3 pm. Telephone: 01434 240459.

- **HOW TO GET THERE:** Falstone is 8 miles west of the B6320 at Bellingham. The Pheasant Inn is at Stannersburn, to the south-east of Falstone Bridge.
- **PARKING:** Roadside parking in Falstone or at the Pheasant, with the permission of the landlord.
- **LENGTH OF THE WALK:** 8 miles from the Pheasant Inn, 6½ miles starting from Falstone or 4 miles from the Hawkhope car park. Map: OL 42 Kielder Water and Forest (Pheasant Inn GR 723866).

THE WALK

1. From the Pheasant turn left then right to Falstone. Passing the Blackcock Inn, go beneath a railway bridge. Turn left along the road then turn left down a rough lane, passing wooden gates. At an intersection with a dolomite track turn left, passing Hawkhope on the left. Keep on past High Hawkhope to Hawkhope car park at the end of the reservoir overlooking the huge dam. Walk along to the end of the car park to an information board. For much of this walk you will follow the orange waymarked Belling Trail.

2. Turn right and enter the trees. Cross a small footbridge and rejoin the dolomite track. Turn left and within a few yards turn left onto a path, which bears right alongside the reservoir. At Gordon's Walls, the former site of a defensive bastle house, keep on across a bridge over Starsley Burn. Follow orange waymarkers and arrows on trees near the edge of the reservoir. Bearing right, the path then crosses a footbridge and follows the inlet. Keep on, passing a sign to Belvedere, then take a left path indicated by an orange marker to a T-junction. Turn left and

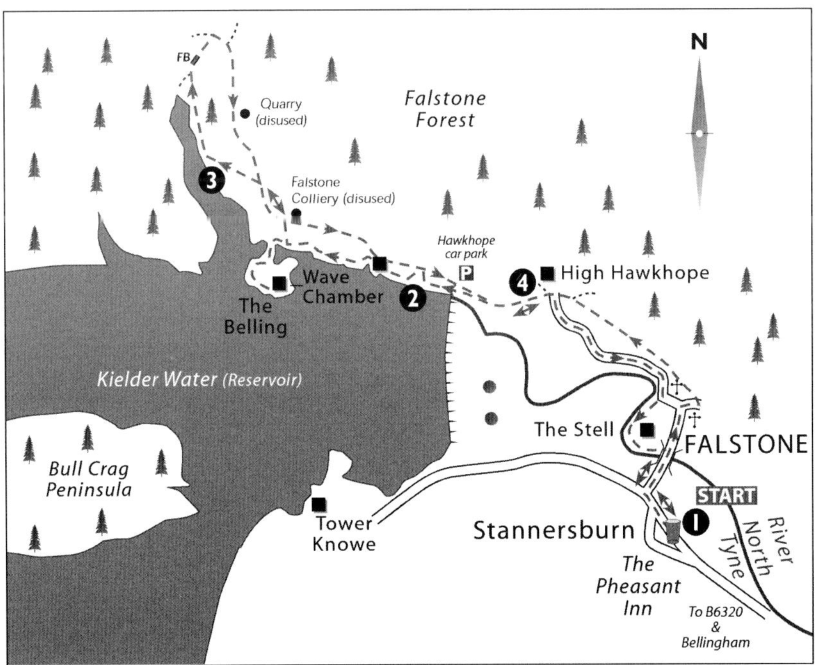

The Wave Chamber at point 2 of the walk

follow the path which winds round the Belling peninsula to the beehive shaped Wave Chamber. Retrace your steps. Back at the original T-junction now turn right and follow the waymarks to join the main track. Turn left and walk along to a large clearing. Reaching a line of telegraph poles, turn left down a path at a yellow waymarker post.

3. Near the water's edge follow the path right. From the woodland edge, markers take you across the slightly boggy area at the end of an inlet to arrive at the banks of a small stream, the Belling Burn, at a footbridge. Cross the footbridge and turn right to a stone bridge. Cross the bridge and keep on to a T-junction where you turn right (following a sign to Falstone/Dam). Stay with the track to pass Falstone Mine and the car park. Continue down the track.

4. At the cross tracks at High Hawkhope turn right past extensive farm buildings, which include the remains of a pele, to a wide gate. Go through and follow an unfenced tarmac road over pasture and a humped bridge to a metal gate. Stay with the road past houses and

Hawkhope Road and continue ahead through a kissing gate. Passing Braeside and Mouseyhaugh, follow the river on your right then a children's play area on the left. Then, approaching cottages, follow the sign 'Riverside Walk' near a picnic table. Walk along the riverside to the public sculpture *Stell* (Colin Wilbourn). Stay on the riverside path to the road bridge. Turn left through a gate and follow the right edge of the field. At a wicket gate adjacent to a field gate on the right, exit onto the road through the field gate (the path would continue through the wicket gate back into Falstone). Turn right and retrace your steps to the Pheasant.

PLACES OF INTEREST NEARBY
Kielder Water has a wide range of recreational opportunities, with something for everyone. **Kielder Castle Forest Park Visitor Centre** is based in a former hunting lodge of the Duke of Northumberland, overlooking Kielder village. It houses a restaurant and a craft and gift shop. It is open daily from Easter to October 10 am to 5 pm. November weekends only 11 am to 4 pm. December daily to Christmas 11 am to 4 pm. There is also **Tower Knowe Visitor Centre** and the **Leaplish Waterside Park**. The two latter centres are linked by the ferry service and they are open daily from Easter to the end of October. The Osprey motor cruiser is an excellent way to see the lake in comfort. Telephone: 01434 250209; www.kielder.org

FELTON/WEST THIRSTON AND THE COQUET

This gentle ramble through rolling Northumbrian countryside starts in West Thirston, just south of Felton Bridge and takes you north to Guyzance Bridge before leading you back through Felton village, once a key point on the old Great North Road. You are never far from the river. There are two stretches of pleasant woodland. The rest of the walk is over fields and by field edges.

Felton Bridge

It was at Felton that troublesome northern barons paid homage to the King of Scotland and provoked King John in 1216 into devastating the area. It was also the centre of the Jacobite rebellion of 1715. John Wesley visited Felton during a missionary tour in 1766 and gave a stirring address to the people but 'very few seemed to understand anything of the matter'.

To the west of the village, just off the route of the walk, is the little

Early English church of St Michael, which was restored with money from the Davison family of Swarland Hall. Alexander Davison was the prize agent of Admiral Lord Nelson and he erected an obelisk near the (now) A1 in 1807 bearing the inscription: 'Not to commemorate the Public Virtue and Heroic Achievements of Nelson, which is the duty of England, but to the Memory of Private Friendship . . . '.

Felton is linked to West Thirston on the south side of the Coquet by two bridges. The rather fine medieval bridge dates back to the 14th century. Alongside it is a modern concrete bridge.

The white, double-bowed Northumberland Arms is an old coaching inn in West Thirston at the bottom of The Peth and just south of the old Felton Bridge. Black Sheep Bitter, Jobling's Swinging Gibbet (Jarrow Brewery) and John Smith's are the ales on offer. There is a restaurant area, a public bar and a lounge area. An extensive range of main courses, a good small portion menu and a range of 'lite bites' are served, followed by home-made desserts. The specials board daily adds some exotic extras, such as marinated beef kebabs on a Mediterranean vegetable couscous finished with mustard dressing, or pan fried duck breast on a bed of braised red cabbage with port and damson sauce. The pub is open 12 noon to 9 pm Monday to Friday and 12 noon to 11 pm Saturday and Sunday. Food is available from 12 noon to 3 pm and 6 pm to 9 pm Monday to Friday and 12 noon to 9 pm Saturday and Sunday. Telephone: 01670 787370.

If you prefer teashops, visit The Cheviot on the north side of the bridges, which is open virtually every day until 5 pm.

- **HOW TO GET THERE:** Felton is on the B6345 to the east of the A1 and 10 miles north of Morpeth. From the north, leave the A1 on the B6345 to cross Felton Bridge and arrive at the Northumberland Arms. From the south, turn off for Felton, then, at the junction with the B6345, turn left to descend the *peth* or bank to the Northumberland Arms.
- **PARKING:** Opposite the Northumberland Arms, with the permission of the landlord. Alternatively, there is roadside parking available.
- **LENGTH OF THE WALK:** 6 miles. Maps: OS 325 Morpeth and Blyth and 332 Alnwick and Amble (GR 185003).

THE WALK

1. From the Northumberland Arms turn right and walk to the bridges. Do not cross but continue down the right side of railings then keep ahead on the woodland path and then a good track. Stay with this Coquet-side track, passing arable fields. At a junction of paths keep left and continue to the end of the field, then along the left edge of the next large field. Enter the next field and follow the obvious track away from the river across a bridge, then rising. Keep on through a wide double gate and along the left edge of the arable field, now high above the river, to reach another gate. Exit onto a road. Turn left and at a junction with a track and farm drive turn left down the farm drive (signed to High Park/Acklington Park). Pass cottages, houses and barns and walk towards High Park farm.

2. Turn right alongside a stone/metal barn with a waymarker on the corner. Cross diagonally left over the farmyard then follow the left field edge along a concrete track. At a metal gate turn right and follow the left edge to the field corner. Turn left through two wicket gates. Follow the right edge of the field then turn right through a gate and follow a woodland path to exit over a step stile into a large field. Cross this (towards the pylons) to a step stile (public byway). Go over this and turn left along the track. At a signpost to Warkworth/Rake Lane turn left, passing Acklington Park Farm to reach a road.

3. Turn left, passing Wellfield House and then an impressive former iron foundry on the left, to cross the fine Guyzance Bridge. The ruins in the field to the right are those of Brainshaugh Chapel. Turn left along the road to another bridge. Cross this then turn left down a track past a memorial to ten soldiers who died in 1945 when floods and currents took them over the weir (constructed by John Smeaton, 1775). Follow the track past Waterside Cottage then right to a ruin and a signpost to Mouldshaugh/Felton. Cross the step stile on the left and keep parallel to the right field edge on a faint track. At the fence corner turn right and continue through four gates, following the right field edge. Go through another gate and follow the next right field edge. At a step stile on the right cross and follow a narrow fenced path alongside a plantation. Go through a wicket gate and into the next field. Follow the left edge and at the end in the left corner cross a step stile and footbridge and keep on with a fence on the right at first. The woodland path is quite narrow and rather overgrown. It leads downhill into the woods and winds on to cross another footbridge (inscribed 'You are never nearer to God than in the heart of a wood').

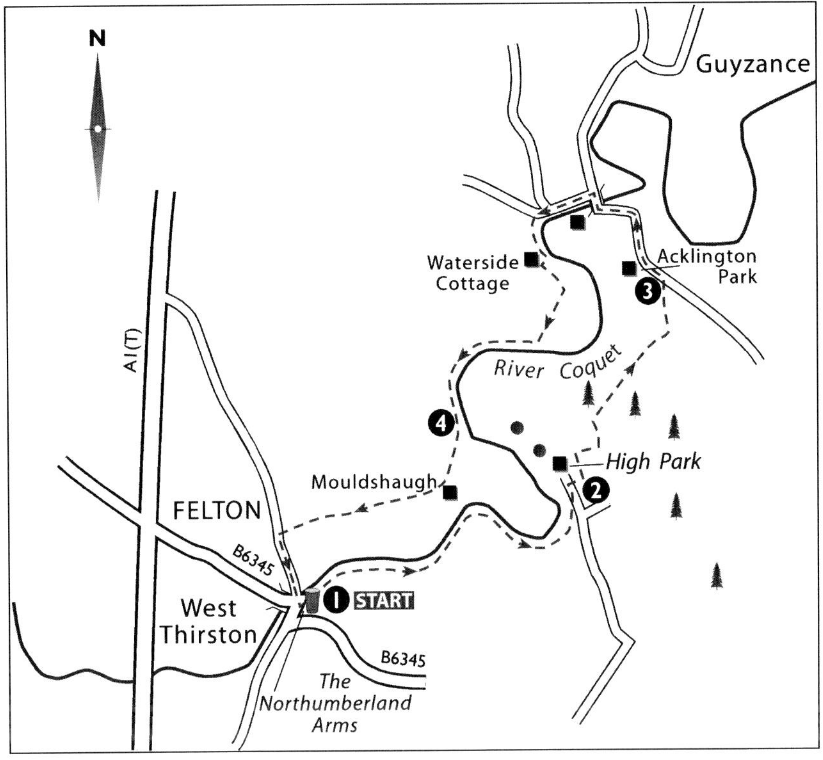

4. Keep on to exit the wood over a step stile into a field. Keep to the left edge to a kissing gate. Go through the gate then cross a footbridge. Ascend a short, steep length of track and walk across a field diagonally right on a clear path to Mouldshaugh Farm. Follow the marker post to a signpost. Turn right for Felton along Mouldshaugh Lane between arable fields. At a fork turn left and keep on to reach the old A1. Turn left down Tomlinson's 'gentle declivity' back to the bridges.

PLACE OF INTEREST NEARBY

Brinkburn Priory (English Heritage) is 9 miles west of Felton on the B6344 (Rothbury Road) off the A1. It is a fully roofed and restored idyllic riverside Augustinian Priory church which is a marvellous example of early Gothic architecture. Telephone: 01665 570628; www.english-heritage.org.uk

WARKWORTH AND THE COQUET

Warkworth, a fine example of a medieval planned town, was laid out near the lowest crossing of the Coquet, which almost encircles it. The skyline is dominated by the splendid castle. This fascinating route includes an unusual fortified bridge and a hermitage carved from solid rock. The common theme is the lovely meandering river.

The fortified bridge at Warkworth seen from the west

Near the start of the walk is the Norman church of St Lawrence, once the scene of the massacre of 300 people when Scottish invaders burnt it with them inside. In 1715 the Jacobites proclaimed the Old Pretender as King in Warkworth. The 1379 fortified bridge is unusual in northern England. The new bridge was built in 1965. The Warkworth Hermitage is a curious chapel carved out of the riverside cliff in the mid-14th century. A rather romantic spot, it has attached to it the legend of a knight who lost his lover in tragic circumstances and blamed himself for her fate. The last hermit lived here in the 16th century. It can be approached by means of an English Heritage ferry (operating April to September, Wednesday, Sunday and bank holiday weekends, 11 am to 5 pm).

The Hermitage Inn overlooks the market cross. Bar meals include dishes such as steak and mushroom pie, fish, gammon steak, roast chicken, home-made lasagne, and liver and onions. The à la carte menu lists Banquet of Lamb Jennings, roast duck, trio of lamb chops, chicken breast, grilled trout and grilled sea bass, amongst others. In addition there is a range of salads, sandwiches and baked potatoes. The real ales on offer are Jennings and John Smith's.

The inn is open from 10 am to 12 pm on Monday to Saturday and 10 am to 11 pm on Sunday. Food is served from 12 noon to 2 pm and 5.30 pm to 9 pm on Monday to Thursday; 12 noon to 9 pm on Friday and Saturday; 12 noon to 2 pm and 5.30 pm to 7 pm on Sunday. There is a carvery on Friday and Saturday nights and Sunday lunchtime. You may need to book at these times. Telephone: 01665 711258.

- **HOW TO GET THERE:** Warkworth is 8 miles south-east of Alnwick on the A1068.
- **PARKING:** Warkworth market square or by the river past the church.
- **LENGTH OF THE WALK:** 4½ miles. OS Explorer 332 Alnwick and Amble (GR 248062).

THE WALK

1. From the Hermitage Inn turn right to the old fortified bridge. Don't cross but turn left along the riverside. When the lane ends keep on along a gravel path (signed to Mill Walk/Howlett Hall). Pass a footpath leading up to the castle, and some boat hire steps. Exit into a meadow via a kissing gate. Keep on to the Warkworth Hermitage ferry steps and a tarmac road. Turn left and walk up the bank then go through a kissing gate at Howlett Hall. Turn left on the minor road and walk to a junction. Turn right along Watershaugh Road. Keep on past a rest home, Coquet Way and Heather Leazes. Descend a pleasant hedged lane. It turns left near a wooden gate and almost hidden in the hedge is a ford warning sign.

2. Just past that follow a path to the right to a footbridge across the Coquet. Cross the bridge and turn left along the riverside path. At the ford turn right up the lane. It bends right at a cottage but keep straight

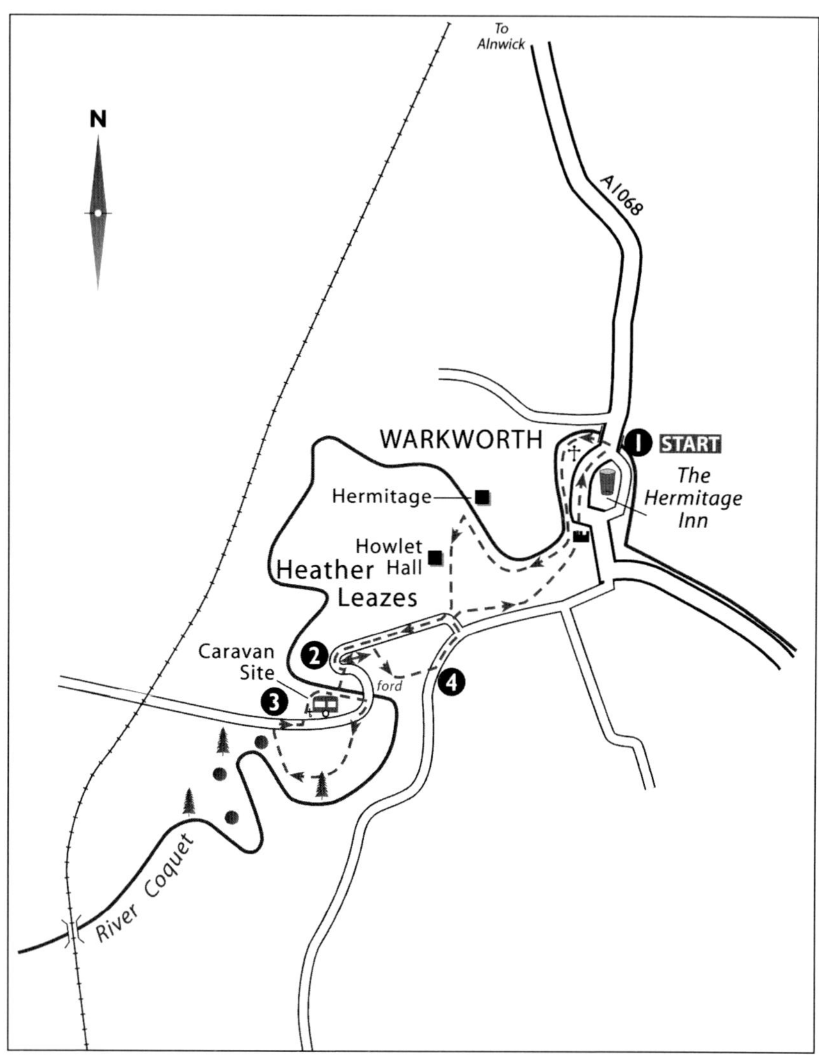

on along a green lane. Go through a wide metal gate into pasture and follow the hedge on the right. Go through another gate then follow the right field edge to exit through a wide gate into a plantation. A left turn would take you down to the Coquet. Turn right along a narrow path and go through a gate onto a lane. Turn right and walk down the lane to a footpath sign on the left to Heather Leazes.

3. Turn left on the narrow enclosed path. Where this ends turn right through a gate into the caravan park. Follow the edge of a copse then keep on the same line across the site to another gate and stile, which take you back onto the riverside path. Turn right and walk back to re-cross the footbridge. Retrace your steps back up to Heather Leazes (opposite a footpath sign) and turn right, following a tarmac lane and then a rough track. At the end turn left along a hedge and through a wide gate. Don't follow the road round to the left but walk into a cul-de-sac and turn right onto a narrow gravelled fenced path. Walk down this to a road.

4. Turn left and walk to a junction then go left along Watershaugh Road. At a sharp left bend keep straight on and almost immediately turn right along a path signed 'Warkworth Castle'. Follow the right field edge on a gravel path. Go through a wicket gate into a children's play area then bear left to go through another kissing gate and keep on over the field towards the castle. Beyond another kissing gate walk along a gravel path to the left of the castle. Descend stone steps into the moat then keep on, ignoring paths to left and right, and rise to an exit at the top of Warkworth's main street.

PLACE OF INTEREST NEARBY

Warkworth Castle is one of the premier castles in the north of England and is in the care of English Heritage. Situated on a prominent hill overlooking the village, with its unusual cruciform shaped keep, curtain walls and towers and heavily fortified gatehouse, it was a very significant Percy stronghold. Open April to September 10 am to 5 pm daily; October 10 am to 4 pm daily; November to March 10 am to 4 pm, Saturday to Monday. Telephone: 01665 711423; www.english-heritage.org.uk

ALNMOUTH AND THE ALN

Walk alongside a scenic harbour, then a stretch of the River Aln to reach the curiously named Lesbury, followed by another riverside path. Leaving the river and walking north-east gives you excellent views over the meandering Aln and its saltmarshes. The final leg takes you past a historic golf club, then by the coastal strand to Alnmouth.

The view of Alnmouth from across the estuary

The Aln flows from near Alnham to Alnmouth. Cheviot rivers are less destructive than those from the Pennines but are more prone to remodel their glacial sediment beds. At Alnmouth the river is notable for its meanders. The Aln is tidal for almost 2 miles upstream from its mouth. Saltmarshes are created by specialised plants that can grow in sediment saturated with salt water. The pre-Roman name is probably the same as for the Alwin and Allen – *white* or *clear* water. It is claimed, incidentally, that Lesbury's name (Lechesbiri in 1190) means physician's or *leeche's* manor.

Alnmouth was founded in 1147. It reached the height of its prosperity in the 18th century as the main port between the Tyne and Tweed, linked by the 'corn road' to Hexham. The harbour held as many as eighteen vessels. In 1779 the American naval commander John Paul Jones paid it the compliment of taking a pot shot at the church as he passed on his way south. Smuggling was also a local business pursued with 'much boldness and success'. John Wesley thought Alnmouth a 'wicked place'. In 1806 a severe storm changed the course of the river, cutting the village off from Church Hill and the old harbour entrance to the south of it. It declined to a small fishing port. However, the railway encouraged the development of a tourist industry; visitors included Charles Dickens. By 1852 one local historian wrote: 'In the summer season the village is filled with the inhabitants of Alnwick and District, who resort to it for sea bathing. The sands are beautifully firm and the adjoining grassy links smooth as velvet carpet in the sunshine of a hot summer's day – most enjoyable.'

William Weaver Tomlinson advised tourists in 1888: 'Alnmouth . . . now one of the most popular of Northumbrian watering-places . . . has many attractions and is . . . within an easy distance of many lovely rural and pastoral scenes and places of historic interest . . . On the smooth, firm sands, or the far-stretching breezy links, where golf, cricket and tennis are played during the summer months, the visitor in search of health will soon realise the benefits of the seaside.'

Alnmouth played a key role in the development of golf. The Alnmouth Golf Club at Foxton Hall, founded in 1869, is the fourth oldest in England and was a major influence upon the game, including the beginning of the Amateur Championship in 1885. The Alnmouth Village Golf Club occupies the original links course.

The Hope and Anchor is claimed to be the oldest building in Alnmouth, and as you would expect there is a good seafood menu here. Other main courses include items such as braised lamb shank with dates, treacle and red wine, grilled rib-eye steak with tomato topped with blue cheese butter and chicken breast in cider apple and cream sauce. There are also salad dishes and a special vegetarian range, as well as various 'light bites' and baguettes. Local ingredients are used and everything is freshly cooked. Real ales from Black Sheep and Hadrian's Border Brewery are featured. A beer garden is available to be enjoyed on fine days. The pub is open from 11 am to 11 pm every day. Food is available from 12 noon to 2.30 pm and 6 pm to 9 pm every day. Telephone: 01665 830363.

- **HOW TO GET THERE:** Alnmouth is approximately 5 miles east of Alnwick. Coming from the south, turn off the A1068 onto the B1338 at the Hipsburn roundabout. Follow this into Alnmouth, turning right at another roundabout. The lane to the Commoner's car park is first left and the Hope and Anchor pub is just after that.
- **PARKING:** Roadside or in Alnmouth Common car park (fee payable).
- **LENGTH OF THE WALK:** 4½ miles. Map: OS Explorer 332 Alnwick and Amble (GR 246106).

THE WALK

1. From the Hope and Anchor turn right and right again down the Wynd past Alnmouth Common car park and onto the beach. Turn right and follow the beach round into the estuary. Cross the dunes and ascend steps onto the road. Turn left and follow the road past a children's grassy play area, Pease's Park. Just beyond this is an electricity sub-station and a path signed meaningfully as Lover's Walk.

2. Turn left down the path, following the estuary edge. At the Duchess's Bridge ascend steps to a road. Cross the bridge and walk along the road. Just before a school turn right through a kissing gate, signed to Lesbury. Follow the right field edge then a line of old hawthorns to exit through a kissing gate. Keep along a grassy path at the bottom of a series of gardens and through another kissing gate. After a few yards the grassy path bears left to a kissing gate. Go through this onto a road. Turn right and cross a footbridge.

3. Turn right and follow the sign to Alnmouth/Foxton Hall. Cross another footbridge and walk along a narrow path into a meadow. The path undulates along the riverbank. At a fence turn right to follow it round. Cross a couple of ladder stiles then a third stile where you turn left and continue alongside a line of telegraph poles up the steep slope to reach a ladder stile. Look back over the extravagantly meandering Aln.

4. Cross the stile and road to walk down the golf club drive. Approaching the clubhouse you have two options. *For the beach route see point 5.* For the higher coastal path turn right at the start of the buildings and follow a sign to cross half left, bearing round a green then over to join an easy track. Where the path meets a wider grassy path turn right, passing caravans, and cross the golf course, keeping

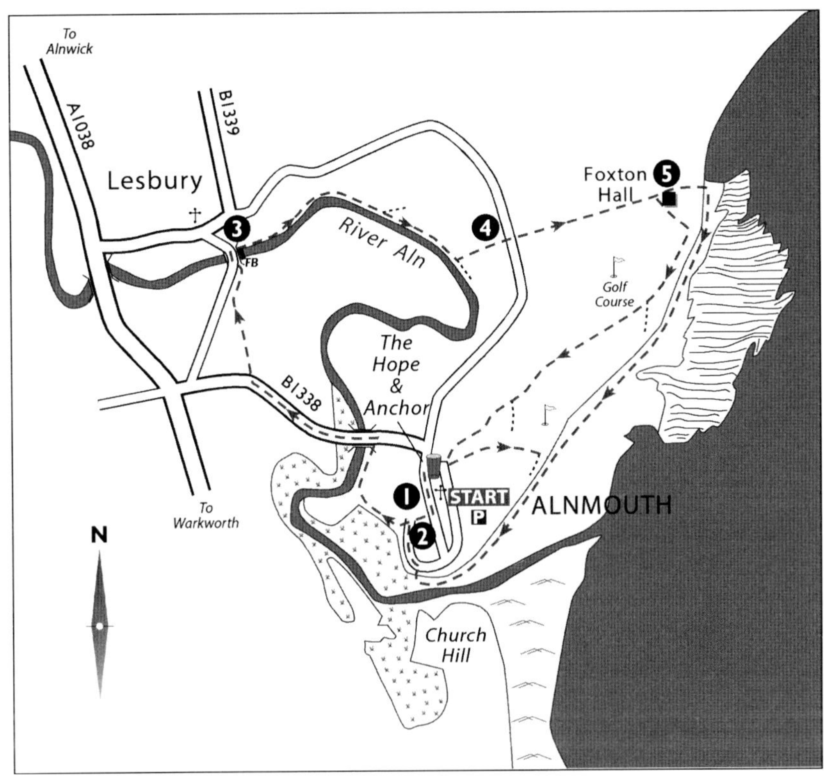

to the right edge and passing a green on your left. Eventually you arrive at a concrete gun battery. Stay on the top track, ignoring other paths to the left. Alnmouth Village Golf Club is below on the left. Alnmouth comes into sight. The path then descends, passing through a small copse of trees and bringing you back to the Wynd.

5. *For the beach route – if passable:* Keep on down to the members' car park and take a path descending on the left side of a wall past the 7th Tee on the right to follow a tree-lined path onto the beach via a gate. Turn right along the beach. At high tide you may need to pick your way along a rocky stretch, crossing limestone ledges on the way, to the sands. Follow the beach back to the car park, passing breakwaters and wartime coastal defence concrete blocks. Walk back up the Wynd to the start.

Looking towards the Duchess's Bridge at point 2 of the walk

PLACE OF INTEREST NEARBY

Alnwick Castle is one of the great fortresses of Europe, and set in a stunning landscape. It has been a film location for many productions, including *Harry Potter* and *Blackadder*. The many attractions and exhibitions include the story of knighthood (. . . and if you are young enough you can dress up, learn to use a sword and face the Quest!). There is also an excellent castle shop and a splendid restaurant. It is open from 10 am to 6 pm daily from Easter to October. Telephone: 01665 510777; www.alnwickcastle.com

The **Alnwick Garden** is one of the most exciting contemporary gardens to be developed in the last century. It is a magical landscape created from unique ideas and has many attractions. It was created with children very much in mind, especially the enormous tree house and the water features. Getting wet is a compulsory part of the programme! The garden is open every day of the year except Christmas Day. Telephone: 01665 511350; www.alnwickgarden.com

ALWINTON AND THE ALWIN

A long and gradual ascent along an antique drovers' road affording spectacular views over Coquetdale and the Simonsides is followed by a descent through tongue-twisting Kidlandlee forest to the banks of the little River Alwin, which you follow back to Alwinton.

The view from Clennell Street looking towards Rookland Hill

The Upper Coquet valley used to be a regular stop for Scottish drovers on their way to the markets at Hexham and Newcastle on a track called Clennell Street. It was also used by shepherds taking sheep to summer pastures and living in temporary shelters or shielings. At Alwinton, Clennell Street meets The Street, which follows the Coquet, here emerging from the hills. The bubbling Alwin runs south from the Cheviots to join the Coquet, which rises further west and traces an eastward course to reach the sea at Amble.

The Rose & Thistle, a former coaching inn, is claimed to have originally been either Rose or Thistle depending on which country controlled the area at the time. There is a bar, a large lounge/restaurant area and a beer garden. Sir Walter Scott penned *Rob Roy* here. Northumbrian Gold Farne Island real ale is on offer. A good range of bar meals is also available, as well as snacks, sandwiches and jacket potatoes and children's favourites. The pub is open from 12 noon to 3 pm and 7 pm to 11 pm on Tuesday to Friday; 12 noon to 5 pm and 7 pm to 11 pm on Saturday and Sunday; 7 pm to 11 pm on Monday. Food is available from 12 noon to 2.30 pm and 7 pm to 9 pm on Tuesday to Saturday and 12 noon to 2.30 pm on Sunday. Telephone: 01669 650226; www.roseandthistlealwinton.com

- **HOW TO GET THERE:** Alwinton is approximately 9 miles north of Otterburn. Turn north-west off the B6341.
- **PARKING:** In the National Park car park (free).
- **LENGTH OF THE WALK:** 7 miles. Map: OL 16 The Cheviot Hills (GR 921063).

THE WALK

1. From the Rose & Thistle turn right to a junction. Follow the signpost to Clennell Street over the village green to cross a footbridge. Turn left at the sign 'Clennell Street/Border Ride', passing a house drive on the right then taking the next right up Clennell Street. Follow this clear track as it rises and winds. At a cottage ignore the marker post and keep on along the grassy path. At a bridleway sign keep left and follow the track as it rises and bends left. Kidlandlee Forest appears ahead. The track descends to a gate. Go through and continue. The track rises again then descends, passing sheepfolds, and you reach a wide gate.

2. Do **not** go through. Follow the right side of a fence through another gate and keep on ahead past a fence corner with woodland very close on the right. Cross a step stile and follow the grassy track to the ruined remains of Wholehope Youth Hostel. In front of these turn right, following a waymarked post, and go through a gate. Head half right, descending to cross a small stream. The path may be very difficult when the vegetation is at its thickest. Aim for the far right corner to exit via a gate onto a track.

3. Turn right for a few yards, then fork left onto a less pronounced grassy track. Keep along this with woodland on your left. Passing a marker post, keep on a few yards then veer right onto a stony track. Turn right and follow the track round to the left to pass isolated

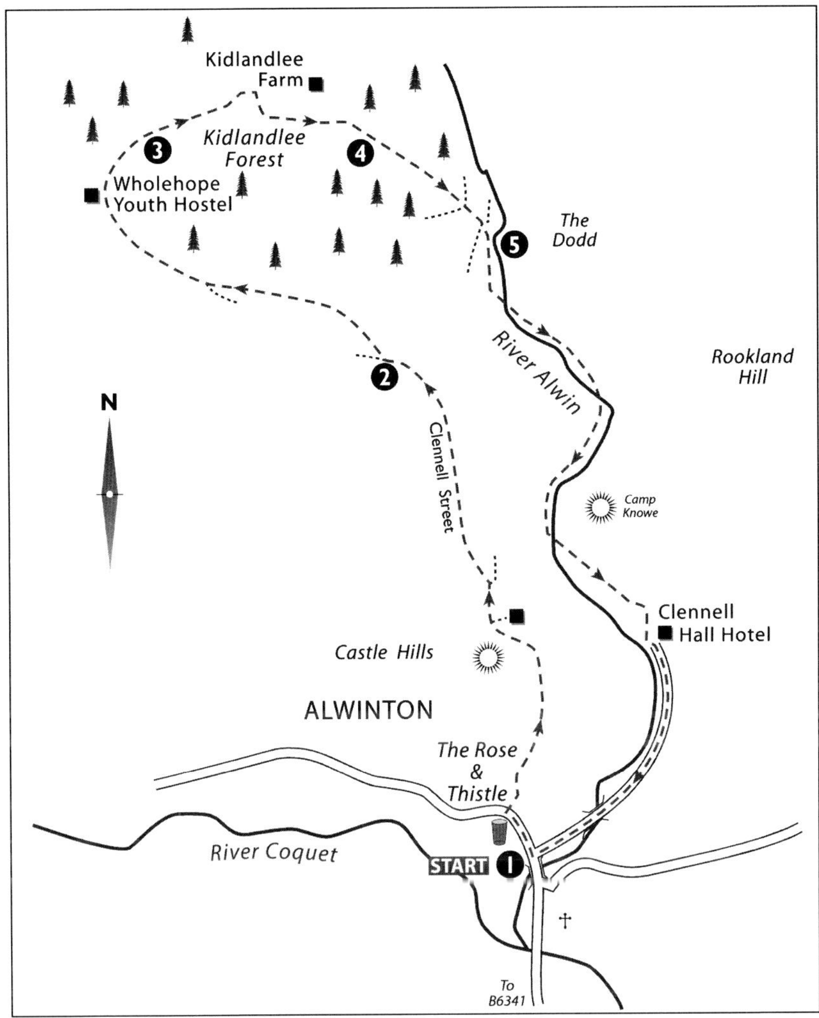

Kidlandlee farm. Continue with a fence on the left. Where the farm drive meets the track, cross a step stile to the right of a gate. Follow the path along a woodland edge on the left to go over another stile.

4. A waymarked post points along a forest path. The path is wide and clear. Descending steadily, you reach a small clearing and another marker post. Veer slightly to the right, passing another marker post, to descend finally down steps onto a wide track. Cross the track to

The Rose & Thistle in Alwinton

follow another marker post down a path through the trees again. Ignoring tracks joining from the right, keep on down the path to a wide track beside a cattle grid and a sign back to Kidlandlee.

5. Turn right along the narrow Alwin valley. You are close to the river all the way. Cross a series of three wide tractor bridges then enter a broad meadow area with Clennell ahead. At a cross tracks keep on through a gate, passing barns on the left and a footbridge on the right. Pass the Clennell Hall Hotel on the left and join a road. Keep on along this with the Alwin now close on the right. Cross a road bridge and follow the unenclosed road over a meadow to exit at a road junction beside a road bridge. Turn right and walk back into Alwinton.

PLACE OF INTEREST NEARBY
Cragside (National Trust) is to the east of Alwinton, a mile north of Rothbury off the B6341. This breathtaking Victorian house and gardens was the creation of Lord Armstrong, the famous Victorian inventor and munitions manufacturer. It was the first house in the world to be lit by electricity. Telephone: 01669 620150; www.nationaltrust.org.uk

WOOLER, THE COLDGATE BURN AND THE CAREY BURN

A wishing well, two lovely rushing burns and an exhilarating return journey across Wooler Common, with a splendid view of the ancient Cheviots to top it all, are all included on this excellent walk from 'windy Wooler'.

Carey Burn viewed downstream from the north

Wooler was originally an agricultural market town but developed in the 19th century as a tourist gateway to the beautiful Cheviots. A local doctor wrote a book of walks in 1926 arguing that a holiday at Wooler was a health cure: 'The kind of case for which Wooler is pre-eminently suited is simply that of the person who is in need of rest and recreation, either in consequence of prolonged overwork, or of illness . . . Wooler is capable of being at once a haven of rest and a cornucopia of fresh vigour . . .'

Its situation on the edge of the Cheviots, and on a railway line from Alnwick to Cornhill, made Wooler a detox Mecca renowned for the 'goat's whey cure'. Sir Walter Scott stayed briefly at a nearby farm in 1791 (because he found the accommodation at Wooler so bad!) and described an Elyssian existence: 'Out of the brooks with which these fields are intersected, we pull trouts of half a yard in length . . . My uncle drinks the whey here, as I do ever since I understood it was brought to his bedside every morning at six by a very pretty dairy-maid . . . all the day we shoot, fish, walk and ride; . . . so much simplicity resides among these hills, that a pen . . . was not to be found about the house . . . till I shot the crow with whose quill I write this letter.'

The Black Bull in Wooler's High Street is a friendly and unpretentious local. The real ales on offer are Young's Waggledance (honey based) and Secret Kingdom (Hadrian and Borders Brewery). There is a good bar meal menu with a wide range of fish dishes and grills – including the challenging Bull Mixed Grill – as well as a vegetarian selection, children's dishes, breakfasts and a variety of jacket potatoes, hot rolls, sandwiches and toasties. The pub is open from 11 am to 11 pm. Food is served from 12 noon to 2.30 pm and 7 pm to 8.30 pm. Telephone: 01668 281309.

- **HOW TO GET THERE:** Wooler stands on the A697 and is approximately 15 miles north-west of Alnwick. From the south following the A697 cross the bridge over Wooler Water, then turn left off the A697 and up into Wooler High Street. The Black Bull is on the right next to the bus station. Ramsey's Lane is practically opposite.
- **PARKING:** Roadside parking at the end of Ramsey's Lane.
- **LENGTH OF THE WALK:** 8½ miles. Map: OL 16 The Cheviot Hills (GR at Ramsey's Lane 986278).

THE WALK

1. Walk up the bridleway towards Wooler Common, passing Waud House, and go through a wicket gate signed to Pin Well. Continue down a grassy path in the pleasant valley, through a wicket gate and into a more open area. Keep right at a fork and on down to the Pin Well, a small marshy area. Go on through a metal gate and along a rocky path. Passing the entrance to a quarry on the left, keep on along the quarry drive to a wicket gate beside a big double gate. Pass through the wicket gate and turn left along a lane. At a T-junction turn right for North Middleton. Follow this quiet lane, passing a couple of lane ends on the right. At a wood on the right and just past a cottage near

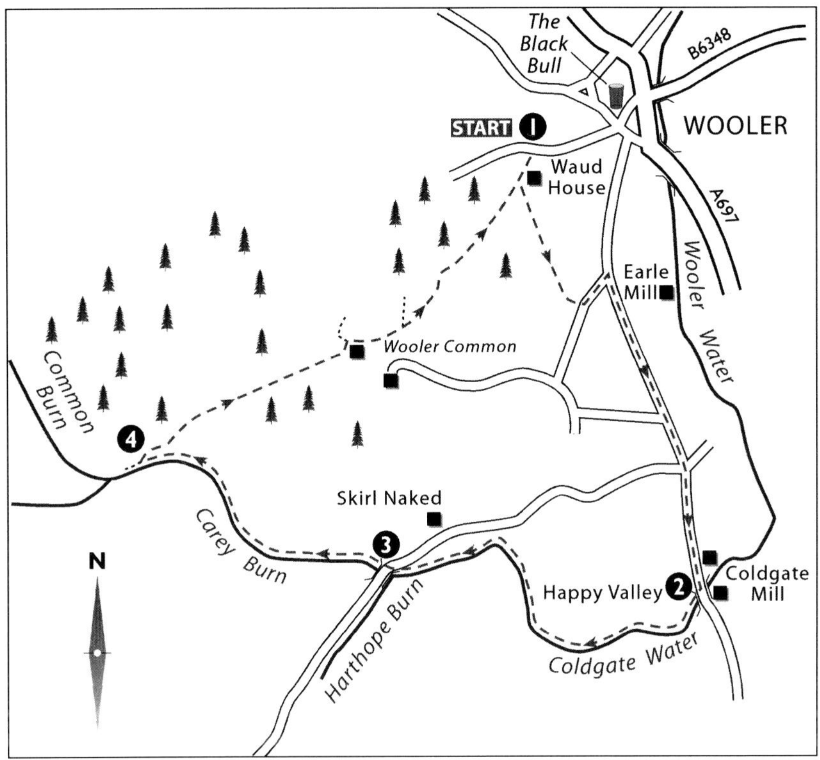

Coldgate Mill on the left, turn right at a sign to Harthope Valley, up a path then through a kissing gate.

2. Stay on this track through the delightful Happy Valley to Carey Bridge with Coldgate Water on the left. The woodland track rises and descends to exit over a step stile into a meadow. Keep on, slightly to the right, then cross another step stile at more woods. Keep along the wood edge with the burn on your left. Cross another meadow, keeping on past a marker post at a cross paths. The path rises uphill through bracken and gorse but is obvious enough. It descends into another open area. Follow the grassy path then cross a stile and keep on into the last meadow area and to a step stile signed back to Coldgate Mill. Cross this and turn left along a road to Carey Bridge, rebuilt in 1956 to replace one swept away by flooding.

3. Don't cross the bridge but go over a step stile at its east end. Follow the burnside path up a rocky bank and turn left where a path is met from the right. Ignore side paths as you go into the narrowing valley. The path rises into a scree area, narrows and becomes rocky. Pass the Carey Burn Linn. Keep on the path across a couple of awkward rocky outcrops, past a timber shelter then on towards woodland. Follow the edge of the plantation and enter it via a step stile. The path crosses timber bridging in places then winds round to meet a bridleway (the ominously named Hellpath) at a T-junction.

4. Turn right and follow the path as it winds to the right of a hill. Keep on through a wicket gate and ahead to a T-junction with a very wide track. Turn right then follow it, crossing three step stiles. Approaching a farm turn left over a step stile signed to Brown's Law/Wooler and follow the wall on the right to cross another step stile, signed to Wooler/Waud House. Turn right here and follow a bridleway parallel to the wall to go through a wide gap in the field corner near a sign to Waud House/Wooler. Aim for the right side of a large plantation to enter it through a wicket gate. Follow the clear woodland path to exit the plantation via a gate. Continue on a grassy path, passing marker posts then reaching a fork. Turn right on the narrow path and follow it down into the little valley, then through a couple of gates to Waud House.

PLACE OF INTEREST NEARBY
Chillingham Castle, east of Wooler off the B6348 south of Chatton, is the most haunted castle in Britain. Since the 13th century it has been continuously owned by the Grey family. The castle has intriguing interiors, arms and armour, a torture chamber, dungeons, Italian ornamental gardens and woodland walks. There are tearooms and a gift shop. It is open at Easter and then from May to September every day except Saturday: grounds and garden from 12 noon to 5 pm; the castle from 1 pm to 5 pm. Telephone: 01668 215359; www.chillingham-castle.com

ETAL AND THE TILL

This delightful route, which starts at the only thatched inn in Northumberland, leads past the cannon protected gatehouse of Etal Castle, then onto the secluded banks of the lovely River Till. Turning eastwards at Tiptoe, the walk takes you along field edge paths to rejoin the riverside.

Etal Castle's gatehouse

Etal was an area seriously affected by border warfare and reiving. Many landowners fortified their manor houses and Etal Castle was crenellated in 1341. It was much involved in the Flodden campaign in 1513, colours taken by the English on that fateful day being deposited at Etal. In the 19th century it had 50 houses and 200 residents and had been even larger when there was a working colliery there. By then it belonged to the Marquis of Waterford and was part of the Ford and Etal estate.

The Till had mills along it for centuries and Heatherslaw Mill is still in operation, connected to Etal by a light railway. The village of Ford came into the possession of the Marchioness of Waterford in 1822 and was remodelled by her successor, Louisa. Towards the end of the century, it was described by William Weaver Tomlinson: ' . . . the cosy-looking, homelike cottages, half hidden in foliage and trimmest of gardens . . . present a picture of rural peace and retirement.' Since 1907 Ford and Etal have belonged to the Joicey family. The first Baron Joicey rose from pit-boy to become one of the most prominent mine owners in the region.

The River Till rises in the Cheviots and flows north to meet the Tweed. It is notoriously dangerous because of its steeply sloping bottom and unstable sandbanks. It is a beautiful river, though, and little disturbed by human activity.

The thatched Black Bull in Etal is a low, whitewashed, attractive inn with a pleasant beer garden. The main beers are John Smith's and Deuchars. A full menu is offered: tempting starters followed by dishes such as deep fried scampi and fresh chips, mince and dumpling, steak and ale casserole, liver and onions, Cumberland sausage and various home-made pies, also a varied vegetarian selection and a good range of children's meals, plus an extensive dessert menu. It is open all day in summer from 11 am to 11 pm, with food all day except Tuesday night. Winter times are 12 noon to 3 pm and 6 pm to 11 pm on weekdays (closed on Tuesday until 6 pm) and until 12 midnight on Saturday and Sunday. Telephone: 01890 820200.

Alternatively, across the road you will find the Lavender Tearooms (telephone: 01890 820777). At Heatherslaw Mill, just a Heatherslaw Light Railway ride away, there is the Heatherslaw Tearoom (telephone: 01890 820737).

- **HOW TO GET THERE:** Etal is on the B6354 south-west of Berwick. Approaching from the south, turn off the A697 north of Wooler. Take a right turn just after Milfield along the B6354 and follow the signs.
- **PARKING:** In the car park next to the castle.
- **LENGTH OF THE WALK:** 6½ miles. Map: OS Explorer 339 Kelso, Coldstream and Lower Tweed Valley (GR 926394).

THE WALK

1. From the Black Bull turn right along the road past Etal Castle. At a sign to Tindal House/Twizel Bridge turn right through a gate onto a cycle track. Follow this, passing a corrugated iron hut with a stone cross in front of it on the left, a gravestone on the right with the initials M.E.J., then a wooden public sculpture bench. Continue on along the river edge past a suspension bridge. The river bends left as you walk through fine, coniferous woodland. Cross a grand wrought iron footbridge over a wide stream and continue on through deciduous woodland. At a point where a wooden fence begins there is a path to the left of it off the track.

2. Follow the path as it rises to a waymarked gate. Go through and follow the path to the left up a steep grassy bank, with a fence and trees on the left, to the corner where there is a waymarked step stile beside a long wall. Cross the stile and turn right. The undergrowth for the next few yards can seem impossible. Keeping the wall on your right, make your way as best you can to the right corner and a wire

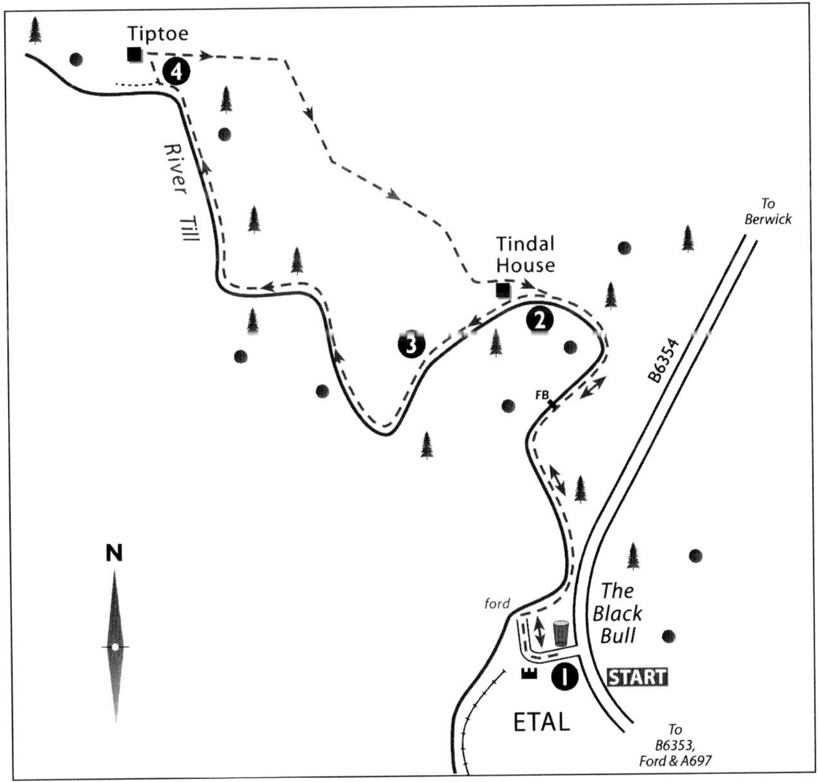

fence. Follow that to a waymark and enter a field. Walk along the left field edge. At the end continue through a gate on the left, hidden by trees, into the next field. Keep on along the left edge of this one. Then exit over a ladder stile in the left corner.

3. Walk downhill with a fence on your left to a step stile into private land. Turn right along the river as it bends to the right. At the end of the meadow follow the path into woodland through a wicket gate and continue on a good path through Black Bank Woods. Keep on along this lovely stretch of river. Exit into a field via a wicket gate. Stay with the river as it bends right. At the end of this field cross a step stile in a wire fence and keep on along an undulating grassy path as it crosses a little stream and a stretch of meadow then goes through a wide gate into deciduous woodland. Keep on past high netting. Where the track forks take the right fork uphill to Tiptoe.

4. Turn right at a signpost for Tindal House. Follow the left edge of a large arable field along a track. Ignore a track leading off to the right. At the end of the field turn sharp right and follow the fenced right edge of another large arable field. At the end of this field go through a gap in the fence then keep on ahead along the right side of the next large field with a hedge to the right. Exit onto a road. Turn right to Tindal Farm. Just before the farm go through the wicket gate on the left onto a National Cycle Network route. Follow the gravel track down to the riverside and retrace your steps to Etal.

PLACES OF INTEREST NEARBY

Amongst many attractions in **Ford** and **Etal** villages is a working corn mill, a narrow gauge light railway, Etal Castle (English Heritage) and the Lady Waterford Hall in Ford, which was decorated with lifesize paintings of biblical scenes by the Marchioness, using local children and adults as models. There is also Ford Nursery in the walled garden of Ford Castle and the Horseshoe Forge Pottery. As if all of that was not enough there is Ford Moss Nature Reserve. Telephone for the Ford and Etal Estates Visitor Centre: 01890 820338; www.ford-and-etal.co.uk

HORNCLIFFE AND THE TWEED

Walk beside the beautiful Tweed to the south of Horncliffe, famous for its chain bridge and its honey farm, to Norham, which is dominated by its romantic castle. The return is along field edges, with some lovely views of the river beneath you.

The Tweed near Horncliffe

Horncliffe is off the beaten track on a red cliff above the Tweed where it ceases to be navigable and tidal near the lowest ford. To the west is scenic Horncliffe Dene, its steep banks covered with ivy, honeysuckle, gorse and trees. In 1820 the ford was superseded by the famous Union Bridge, the first suspension bridge in the UK.

Norham Castle was a popular subject for Turner. It guarded a key ford over the Tweed. For many years Norhamshire belonged to the Bishop of Durham, hence the grandeur of St Cuthbert's church. At Norham, Edward I declared himself Paramount King of Scotland and chose John Baliol from thirteen claimants. The castle was involved in numerous sieges and campaigns and is featured in *Marmion* by Sir

Walter Scott. The quiet village has the appearance and feeling of a Scottish settlement.

The Fishers Arms is a small, whitewashed inn. Main beers are John Smith's and Deuchars IPA and a guest ale. There is a good range of lunchtime 'Light Bites'. Main courses available at lunchtime or in the evening include breaded scampi, steak and ale pie, Cumberland sausage ring, button and porcini mushroom lasagne, chunky vegetable pie and macaroni in a cheese and leek sauce. The pub is renowned for its beer battered local haddock, which is usually available daily on the specials board. There is also a children's menu. Main ingredients are sourced locally, if possible.

The opening times are from 12 noon to 3 pm and 6.30 pm to 10.30 pm on Monday, Wednesday, Thursday and Sunday (closed all day on Tuesday) and the same on Friday and Saturday but closing at 11 pm. Meals are served from 12 noon to 2 pm and 6.30 pm to 8.30 pm, lunchtime only on Sunday. Telephone: 01289 386866.

- **HOW TO GET THERE:** Horncliffe is 5 miles south-west of Berwick off the A698. Heading from Cornhill to Berwick on the A698, pass a left turn to Norham (the B6470), then take the next left and fork right to Horncliffe. The Fishers Arms is in the Main Street.
- **PARKING:** Roadside parking in Horncliffe.
- **LENGTH OF THE WALK:** 5½ miles. Map: OS Explorer 339 Kelso, Coldstream and Lower Tweed Valley (GR 928498).

THE WALK

1. From the Fishers Arms, walk into Horncliffe village square then right past the Old Schoolhouse. Pass a couple of houses and turn right down hedge-lined steps (signed to Norham). Follow the path as it descends then crosses a footbridge at Horncliffe Dene. Ascend a long flight of steps and follow the path round through woods then past a bench with a lovely view over the Tweed. Keep on, passing a step stile on the left, then follow the grassy path down a slope and steps to a ladder stile. Cross this then another in the field corner to reach the Tweed.

2. Turn left and follow an obvious riverside path. Keep on past a ruined fishing hut. Posts indicate fishing beats. The path is joined by a good cart track from the left. Continue along the riverside. Norham Castle appears on the horizon above trees. Keep on, winding to the

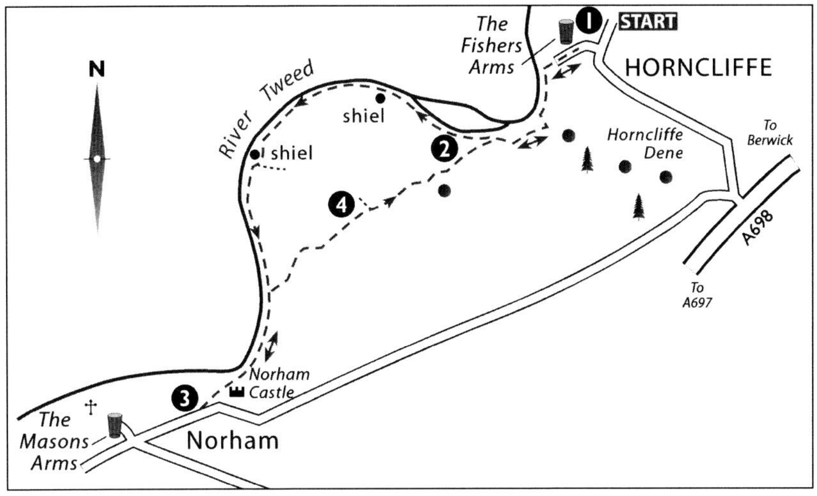

right around a couple of shiels still in use. The path reaches the end of the fields and rises past an old corrugated hut. Leave the riverside and enter the woodland. Cross a ladder stile. Now follow the path past crags, across a footbridge, up and down steps and over a ladder stile. Pass a waymarked post then cross a bridge (remember this point for your return). Keep on across another bridge then down to the riverside. Exit into a field over a ladder stile then bear round left to a kissing gate onto the road into Norham. Here you could visit the Mason's Arms, a small local with genuine character. Telephone: 01289 382326.

3. The return is back through the kissing gate and on to the footbridge with the waymarked post. Follow the arrow uphill along a rough path, which winds up a little dene to a step stile. Cross the stile and follow the left edge of the field. At the end of the field cross a step stile on the left, turn right and follow the fence to cross another step stile. Then head up to the right to cross another step stile into a field. Follow the left field edge. Arriving at a single hawthorn tree on the left, cross a step stile beside it (down in a dip). Keep on along the right field edge. Go over a step stile onto a track and then another into the next field.

4. Cross the middle of this field, or go round the edge if necessary, then go over another step stile into the next field. Here bear half left

The Union Bridge, the U.K.'s first suspension bridge

across to the far left corner. You can see Horncliffe now. Arriving at a gate and a stile in a nettle ridden area in a fold in the ground, cross the stile then bear half right up into trees and up a slope to a fence. Follow the fence on your right to a hedge then follow the hedge as it turns left then sharp right. Go over a step stile through a hedge and keep on along the left edge of a field to arrive at a stile in the field corner, next to a gate. Cross this then turn right. Now retrace your steps to Horncliffe past the bench and Horncliffe Dene.

PLACES OF INTEREST NEARBY

The opening hours for **Norham Castle** are restricted so you are advised to contact English Heritage for details. Telephone: 01289 304493; www.english-heritage.org.uk

If romantic ruins aren't your scene, visit the **Chain Bridge Honey Farm**. There you will find a honey and beekeeping museum, an observation hive, marvellous murals, a vintage vehicle collection and a unique café in a restored vintage double decker bus. It is accessible from the A698 Berwick to Coldstream road, a mile from the A1 East Ord roundabout. Free admission. Telephone: 01289 386362; www.chain bridgehoney.co.uk

BERWICK AND THE TWEED

Walk along the historic ramparts of Berwick, with excellent views of the historic town and the scenic coast, then cross the famous old Berwick Bridge — try counting the arches — to follow the banks of the Tweed with its swans, salmon and variety of bridges.

Old Berwick Bridge

The only part of England on the north side of the Tweed, Berwick's strategic situation meant that it changed hands thirteen times before becoming finally English in 1482. It is famous for its Elizabethan defences based on an Italian design, built of stone and filled with earth. They were never tested because after 1603 the Border disappeared. Berwick is also notable for the first purpose-built barracks in Britain (Vanbrugh, 1721) and Holy Trinity church, which is one of only two churches built during the Commonwealth period in England.

The Tweed has played an important part in the regional economy. Until the early 20th century salmon fishing was a major industry with the fish being exported in the famous Berwick smacks, the fastest vessels on the east coast. The Tweed has also been an obstacle to be crossed. Berwick Bridge, the oldest, was built between 1611 and 1634 with money granted by James I. In 1928 it was joined by the Royal Tweed Bridge. The Royal Border Bridge, a railway viaduct bridge designed by Robert Stephenson, was built between 1847 and 1850.

The Queen's Head is an old inn not far from the Old Bridge. It serves panninis, baked potatoes and ploughman's at lunchtime, with an imaginative range of fillings. An extensive menu is available in the evening and includes dishes such as fillet steak with bacon, mushroom and thyme sauce; whole lemon sole and nut brown butter; drake duck breast with sticky mango glaze; sliced aubergine courgettes and tomato with houmous; and venison escalope with peppercorn sauce. The bar is open daily from 12 noon to 3 pm and 6 pm to 11 pm. Lunch is available from 12 noon to 2.30 pm and evening meals from 6 pm to 9.30 pm. Telephone: 01289 307852.

If it's real ale you want, visit Barrels Alehouse near the north end of the Old Bridge. In a setting of real character you will find a range of half a dozen real ales such as Wylam Brewery Landlord's Choice, Pentland IPA and Edinburgh Gold.

- **HOW TO GET THERE:** There are several routes into Berwick from the A1. Approaching on the A698 or the A1167 from the south, cross the Royal Tweed Bridge and turn left into Marygate, then through Scots Gate. Approaching from the north along the A1167 or A6105, come down Castle Gate and turn left just before Scots Gate. If you want to start from the Queen's Head, walk down Marygate to the town hall, then turn right down Hide Hill and Sandgate. The Queen's Head is on the right.
- **PARKING:** Below the ramparts outside Scots Gate (pay and display).
- **LENGTH OF THE WALK:** 6½ miles, including the ramparts, or 4½ miles for the riverside walk only. Map: OS Explorer 346 Berwick-upon-Tweed (Queen's Head GR 999526).

THE WALK

1. From the Queen's Head on Sandgate turn left and walk up to a left turn along Bridge Street. Continue straight ahead past Barrels on the left and the Old Bridge, and keep on to exit into Golden Square with the Royal Tweed Bridge on the left. Turn right and walk up Golden Square, then turn left up onto Megs Mount to start your walk around the ramparts. Now you follow the tarmac walkway past the Cumberland Bastion and then the Brass Bastion at the northern corner of the town. Beyond here, after about 100 yards, a path descends to The Parade by the corner of the parish church graveyard. Visit the barracks and the church then continue back along the ramparts, passing the Windmill Bastion and the site of an older fort from the time of Edward VI. Beyond Kings Mount the ramparts rise above the Tweed estuary then turn upriver past Coxon's Tower. Pass some fine Georgian terraces and walk on above the old quay to leave the ramparts walk at Bridge End. Cross the Old Bridge.

2. Turn right past the fine war memorial. Walk along the edge of the river on a tarmac path across an area laid out with picnic tables. Continue beneath the Royal Tweed Bridge then to a road alongside parking bays. Walk on beneath the Royal Border Railway Viaduct, towards old concrete tank obstacles and along a narrow path between them, then by the bank side. It widens into a rough meadow. Stay on the left side to a kissing gate then carry on at the edge of the next field. Through

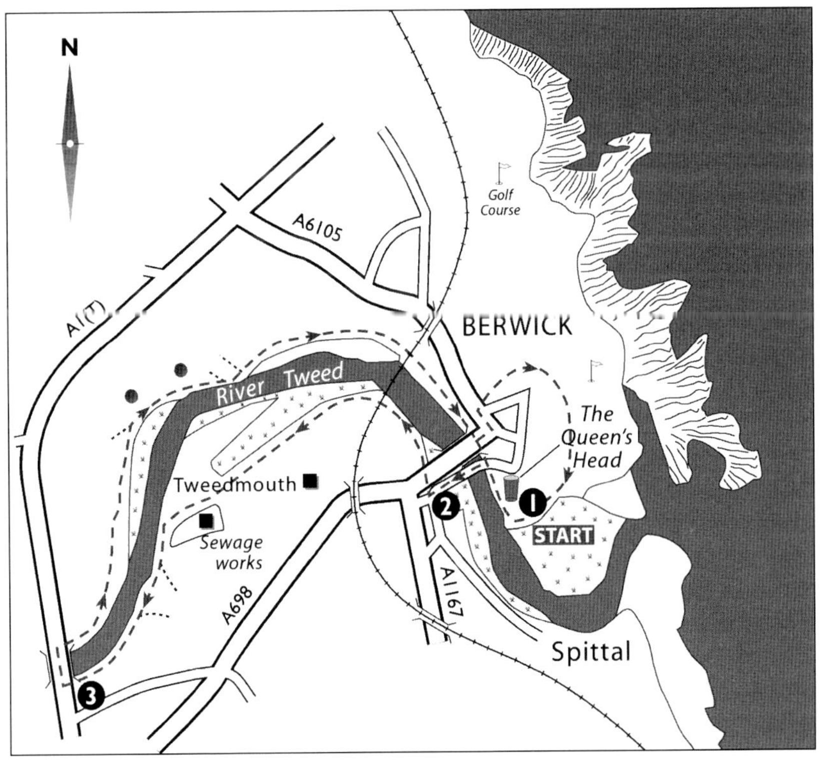

Part of Berwick's ramparts

another gate the path skirts a water treatment plant. Turn left through a third gate and join a tarmac track where you turn right. At a bend about 40 yards ahead bear right along a field edge rising above the steep river bank then continue into the next field. At the end of this look out for a stepped path descending to a stream and a wooden footbridge. Cross this then ascend to a stile beyond and turn right onto the main road.

3. Walk over the bridge, which carries the bypass road. At a sign to Berwick by the Plantation, go right onto a path and follow it across two stiles onto a riverside pasture. Follow the left edge of this for about ½ mile and then, when you cross the head of a stream, bear away from the hedge over towards the river on the right at the base of a wooded bank. You cross a footbridge then bear right to a stile. Ascend the path and, at a junction at the top of the bank, turn right and follow the path until eventually you descend from the wood beside a cottage. From here simply follow the promenade back to Berwick.

Places of Interest Nearby

Berwick Barracks are now home to several museums and exhibitions. **Berwick Borough Museum** provides a kaleidoscope of experiences through *Window on Berwick*. The **King's Own Scottish Borderers' Regimental Museum** illustrates the proud history of one of the great British regiments. Telephone: Borough Museum and Art Gallery 01289 301869; KOSB 01289 307426.